Hug Your Haters

ALSO BY THE AUTHOR

Youtility

Hug Your Haters

How to EMBRACE COMPLAINTS and KEEP YOUR CUSTOMERS

Jay Baer

PORTFOLIO / PENGUIN

PORTFOLIO / PENGUIN
An imprint of Penguin Random House LLC
375 Hudson Street
New York, New York 10014
penguin.com

Foreword by Tom Webster published by arrangement with the author

Photograph on page 113 courtesy of Subaru of Wichita

ISBN 978-1-101-98067-5
Printed in the United States of America

1   3   5   7   9   10   8   6   4   2

Set in Sabon LT Std
Designed by Alissa Theodor

For Alyson, Annika, and Ethan

CONTENTS

FOREWORD

by Tom Webster, Edison Research

I n my business—consumer insights—I get all kinds of requests. Some clients ask me to "prove *x*" for them. Those kinds of requests, to paraphrase A. E. Housman, use research like a drunkard uses a lamppost: for support rather than illumination. But all market research can essentially be boiled down to three categories: comparative research ("how are we doing?"), firefighting ("what the heck do we do?"), and "blue sky" research ("what *could* we do?"). The latter is my favorite type of project because we get to be involved in the discovery of new facts and the exploration of the undiscovered opportunity.

It is, in fact, this undiscovered opportunity that my friend Jay Baer has set out to explore, on your behalf.

When Jay first approached me and my company, Edison Research, he had two provocative questions: How has the proliferation of social media, review sites, and other online forums changed consumer expectations of what "good customer service" really means? When interactions between brands and humans are played out on a public stage, how must brands "perform" in order to satisfy not only the customer but the customer's audience?

With our help, Jay set out to discover the answers to these questions, and many more, in order to provide illumination, not support. Together, Jay and Edison designed a significant national research study to examine current expectations of customer service, how they differ by channel, and the value of responding to complaints, even when those complaints seem unresolvable.

The answers surprised us all. To Jay's endless credit, the book he thought he might write turned out to be a very different book indeed—and a very, very powerful one. The results of the study challenged my own preconceptions about responding to online complaints, and caused me to rethink even how my own business chooses to respond, or not, to "haters."

And here's something that might unsettle you: your business has haters, too. Every interaction between brand and human has the potential to delight or enrage—in short, to become memorable. Today, with the widespread usage of social media, those memories can live on, and live in public, for a very long time. Customer service has become a spectator sport, and your online panel of judges can award or deduct points for speed, execution, and style.

Because that spectator sport can become ugly, many businesses essentially opt out of the game, figuring that it's rigged. I know that was my inclination before Jay embarked on this exploration. But I was wrong. It doesn't matter how rigged the game may seem, how vitriolic the haters may be, or how futile it may seem to please them. The game is worth playing.

You might be tempted to write off "Hug your haters" as a trite saying, a Zen koan, or a beatitude for our digital times. But in the pages that follow, you won't find cherry-picked anecdotes or "feel good" mantras imploring you to turn the other cheek. Jay does not argue from anecdotal information, but from research. And he provides context for that research from some of the world's most successful brands and small businesses, and shows how they have made hugging their haters a systematic process, with tangible results. Jay offers some remarkable case studies of hater hugging and the hard-dollar value that this practice brings to companies that embrace . . . embracing.

What I hope you get from this book is what I got from this book: a change in mind-set. Hugging your haters takes some work. You might be tempted to think about the effort required to monitor and respond to complaints in social media, review sites, and online message boards as a "loss center," a cost of doing business. What Jay convincingly argues, however, is that hugging your haters is not a cost. It's a profit center. Hugging your haters makes good business sense. It's worth it to do the work, because the work pays off. And the most successful "hater huggers" have a competitive advantage and a true strategic moat against their competitors.

I hope this book has the kind of impact on you that it did on me. And if it does, may I humbly suggest one simple thing: when you finish this book (for the first time), log on to Twitter, Facebook, Yelp, TripAdvisor, Amazon, or anywhere else your company has been hated and hug your most recent hater.

Doesn't that feel better?

Hug Your Haters

Introduction

In business and in life, each of us is confronted with people who are perturbed, displeased, disappointed, or downright angry. These people take the time to complain, and let us know where and how we fell short in their eyes.

They are the haters. Their intentions may vary, but there are more of them than ever, and they are louder than ever. And that's good news.

Indeed, what you'll discover in this book is that the rise of the haters is an enormous opportunity for businesses and companies of every type and every size. I've seen this firsthand, as an adviser to some of the world's largest companies and an investor in many small start-ups. Business is more competitive than it's ever been, at every turn and in every way, and differentiation is tough, as competitors can and will eventually mimic your products and ape your pricing. But customer experience and customer service remain fertile opportunities for standing above the mass of competitors. I wrote this book to help all business owners and managers understand how to turn customer service into marketing, and use it as your true competitive advantage.

You may be thinking that this book is unnecessary. You're already

wonderful to your customers. After all, according to a study by Forrester Research, 80 percent of businesses believe they deliver "superior" customer service.[1]

But that same study shows that just 8 percent of customers agree
that service is superior.[2]

As you'll see in these pages, yesterday's great is today's mediocre.
What previously would have been considered adequate attention to
complaints and haters can now become a major customer experience
deficiency that can be exploited by your competitors.

You may be thinking that you already know everything there is to
know about customer service, especially if you are actively involved in
interacting with your customers every day. And a few years ago, you
probably would have been correct. Customer service changed little
between the invention of the toll-free phone number in the 1970s and
the embrace of e-mail as a contact mechanism in the late 1990s.

The same is true in the field of customer service books and counsel. There are dozens of books on the shelves about customer service,
and I cite some of them here. But many of those books, while interesting and worthy of praise, are not relevant in the way they once
were. Mobile and social technology, sociological and behavioral changes,
and heightened consumer expectations have radically shifted what it
means to provide great customer service, and the resources and processes you need to do so.

Hug Your Haters is the first-ever book about *modern* customer
service.

You may also be thinking that you already have a good solution
to haters . . . simply ignore them. Your business is successful. Your
business has always been successful, and you've used the same
approach to complaints and customer service the whole time. Why
change? If it ain't broke, don't fix it.

But it is broken. It has always been broken, we've just chosen not
to admit it to ourselves. A 2013 "Customer Rage" study by Arizona
State University says it best: "Even though companies have substan-

tially increased their spending on handling customer complaints (billions of dollars annually on call centers, enhanced remedies, expanded internet access, etc.), complainant satisfaction in 2013 is still no higher than in the 1970s. Most complainants are dissatisfied with how their customer problems are being handled."[3]

Think about that. *Most* complainants (haters, in the parlance of this book) are dissatisfied with how their customer problems are being handled. For the majority of businesses, the only reason we can eke by with our current customer service approach is because our competitors are equally shabby, or worse.

Why do we so often tell the tales of the legendary, great providers of customer service? Why are case studies from Zappos, Nordstrom, and Ritz-Carlton such a shopworn trope? Why do we constantly reference a tiny, familiar menagerie of companies that we've all agreed "do it right" in customer service? It's because they *are* different. And they are rare. They have made an organizational commitment to provide superior customer experiences, and succeed at differentiating from their competition as a consequence of that emphasis. Does Zappos sell better or cheaper shoes and clothing than competitors? No. Does Nordstrom? No. Does Ritz-Carlton provide demonstrably better accommodations than other high-end hoteliers? No. But each company uses customer service as a wedge to separate it from similar providers of goods and services.

You can do that, too. In these pages, you'll find examples and case studies of small and large businesses, many unfamiliar to you, that understand how customer service has fundamentally changed. They understand how customer service is continuing to change even as you read this. And they understand how smart companies are keeping their customers and outflanking their competition by using the principles and playbooks in *Hug Your Haters,* the most important of which is this:

Haters are not your problem. . . . Ignoring them is.

The tendency of almost everyone (including me) is to turn away from haters. To dismiss their complaints as outliers that are not representative of reality. When confronted with negativity, our instinct is to "turn the other cheek," to quote an ancient source, or to "ignore the trolls," to quote modern packaging of the same advice.

But today this is the wrong approach, because in an era when much of customer service has become a spectator sport, choosing to stay silent actually speaks volumes. As Dave Kerpen, CEO of Likeable Media and author of *Likeable Social Media,* says, "Not responding is a response. A response that says 'I don't care about you.'"

Like selling a stock when its value has dropped, staying silent locks in your losses and ensures that your business will not benefit from a complaint—or your response.

"Nothing ever gets better when you don't address it, and yet in this day and age we still see businesses that don't respond," says George Klein, CEO of customer service mobile app company Peoplocity.

The same shift toward public customer service interactions that has made this book necessary also makes it psychologically difficult to engage with haters, especially when they shine a giant spotlight on their perceptions of your shortcomings. Here's an example of when the outlandish nature of the complaint from a hater would make you want to not respond.

Yelp is a popular feedback and recommendations website where consumers can review and rate all manner of local businesses. This is a Yelp review that is closer to Greek tragedy, written about a Chicago-area location of the White Castle hamburger restaurant chain, which is popular in the central United States:

While driving to the airport near the end of our Midwestern journey, I heard what appeared to be hyperventilating coming from the back seat of our rental car. My 16-year-old son could not believe he was actually seeing a real live, bona fide White Castle, and he begged us to go in. Since we were

> *pretty early for our flight, we decided to go ahead and let him have his "Harold & Kumar go to White Castle" moment, a movie which he asserts is the greatest stoner film ever. Stoner Film, like there's a category for it at Sundance.*

Seems like a positive review at this point. But it takes a decided turn for the worse:

> *I cannot believe that these people actually exchange real American currency for this square, steamed mixture of rodent feces and sawdust on a tiny bun. This is the bastard love child of a 7-Eleven microwavable meat patty and the entrail drippings of roadkill left to fester on Midwestern highways in the hot July sun. Happily it's as thin as a Post-it note so as not to avoid inadvertently engaging your gag reflex.*[4]

Remarkably, on a five-star scale, this is a TWO-STAR review! I desperately want to know what this person writes when he has a one-star experience. In this case, the White Castle restaurant did not respond to the complaint, and perhaps you would have handled it the same way. Don't feed the trolls, right? But it *should* have responded, and so should you in any similar scenario. Answering a review, even one as pointedly negative as this one, increases customer advocacy and shows all onlookers that you do in fact care about your customers. You must hug your haters.

Says Scott Wise, owner of the fourteen-location Scotty's Brewhouse chain of brewpubs, "People don't complain just to complain, they have a legitimate concern, and you need to recognize that as an opportunity, not a problem. My dad taught me the phrase isn't 'We have a problem,' it's 'We have an opportunity to improve an experience.'"

Wise is exactly correct. And even though the number of complaints they have to deal with is far larger, certain big companies are also starting to understand the opportunity value of addressing all complaints. Dan Gingiss is formerly the head of digital customer experience at Discover Financial Services (best known for the Discover card), where he helped transform the service culture to fit modern customer expectations. He warns not to be afraid of complaints. "Not only is a complaint an opportunity to show your great service, but it's an opportunity to figure out the root cause of what is causing irritants with your product or service," Dan says. "It's truly the voice of the customer. Eliminating fear of complaints really changes how you respond to them."

Eliminating fear, especially of public responses to public complaints, and then answering those complaints is an opportunity. In fact, it's quite possibly the single greatest opportunity you have to keep your customers and grow your business. And I can say that not as my own opinion but as a fact, based on proprietary research that determined the precise impact of the methods you'll discover in *Hug Your Haters*.

In this book, you'll learn who complains, why they complain, and how to capitalize on those complaints. We'll also explore why interacting with all haters provides enormous benefits, and what's holding most companies back from doing just that.

In the first chapter we'll look at the specific benefits of increasing your focus on customer service and customer experience.

In chapters 2, 3, and 4 we'll learn about the different types of haters, what they want from you, and where you can have the greatest impact.

In chapter 5 we'll examine the reasons why businesses are not putting emphasis on customer service (especially online), and how to address these issues.

In chapters 6 and 7 we'll learn the precise frameworks for how to handle complaints online and offline.

And in chapter 8 we'll discuss the future of customer service, evaluate new trends that will continue to change how service is provided, and describe what great service requires.

The back of the book includes a quick reference guide, so that you can easily refer back to key statistics and main points once you've finished reading. *Hug Your Haters* is intended to be a book that changes your thinking, but also a resource to which you can refer again and again.

This book was written for you.

This book was written for anyone and everyone who has customers anywhere on the planet. Big companies or small. Business-to-business and business-to-consumer companies. Governments. New companies or old. You'll learn how to hug your haters, embrace complaints, and keep your customers. Doing so turns service into your best competitive advantage while increasing customer retention and company profits.

Chapter 1

Why You Should Embrace Complaints

As Tom Webster explained in his fine foreword to this book, I partnered with his firm—the highly respected attitude collection group Edison Research—to take a close look at the current state of hate. We discussed customer service expectations and outcomes with more than two thousand American consumers who have complained about a company in the previous twelve months, with the study participants representing a statistically valid cross-section of ages, incomes, racial makeups, and technology aptitudes.

And what we found shocked us, both in its comprehensiveness and in its simplicity: *Answering complaints increases customer advocacy across all customer service channels.* In some more than others, and we'll explore that in great depth in this book. But the effect is present in every venue where you interact with customers. If you answer complaints anywhere, it increases advocacy. It takes a bad situation and makes it better.

Conversely, *not answering complaints decreases customer advocacy across all customer service channels.* In some channels more than others, based on traditions and corresponding expectations. But the negative effect of staying silent is also universal. When you don't answer complaints—even in the venues where lack of response is more common (like online review sites)—customer advocacy decreases. It takes a bad situation and makes it worse.

We'll examine the specific benefits of responding to complaints on a channel-by-channel basis when we look at the Hatrix in chapter 3. But for now, consider this: customers feel better whenever and wherever you respond, and they feel worse whenever and wherever you don't. Our exclusive research found that answering complaints has a massive, consistent, and linear relationship to customer satisfaction or dissatisfaction. What else could you possibly do as a business that would produce similar results across the board, other than perhaps dramatically raising or lowering prices?

So what does this research and the more than fifty interviews conducted for this book produce? The Hug Your Haters success equation:

Answer every complaint, in every channel, every time.

In *every* channel. This concept of interacting with customers in the venues they prefer is a critical part of the Hug Your Haters approach. It's about respecting the customers' right to select their own feedback mechanism and approaching customer service accordingly.

"I think that philosophically all channels are important. We should be channel agnostic in terms of feedback. Whether it's a complaint or a compliment or a question, we should interact wherever the customer wants," explains Dan Gingiss.

Admittedly, it's not easy to hug your haters. It takes cultural alignment, resource allocation, speed, a thick skin, and an unwavering belief that complaints are an opportunity. But there are businesses that are already living by the rules of *Hug Your Haters,* and I hope you'll join their ranks when you finish this book. You'll also be able to continue learning (including access to free bonus content that didn't fit inside the book), participate in workshops and webinars, interact with peers, and share your own experiences by visiting HugYourHaters.com. Please join me there when you're ready.

Let's look at two companies, one large and one smaller, that embrace complaints and customer feedback, and examine the impact this approach has on their businesses.

How Fresh Brothers Pizza Hugs Their Haters

Debbie Goldberg is the co-owner of Fresh Brothers Pizza, a thirteen-store chain in Southern California that is committed to responding to all customer feedback—positive and negative. This is a particularly unusual approach on Yelp, where public responses from businesses to customer complaints are still rare, and replies to customer compliments are even less common. But Debbie is heavily involved there, and includes her real e-mail address in every public response to customer feedback.

"I try to answer every Yelp review. I'm a little behind right now, but I'm catching up," she says. "But I think it's important that people know there's a real person behind this company, and because we've grown really quickly, sometimes people think we're just another quick service chain, that there really isn't a face or a family behind the business."

Debbie is masterful at how she handles the haters on the Yelp platform, where twelve of her locations maintain a four- out of five-star average, and one is at three and a half stars. There aren't many negative reviews for Fresh Brothers, but this one received a typical and illustrative reply from Debbie.

From Ray S. from Los Angeles (a one-star review):

Cardboard!! Think Cardboard with cheese. That's about it! When they say toppings, they are non-existent. Maybe the others writing reviews don't know what great pizza taste like but this is not. No toppings what so ever! What a disappointment.

> *We also tried some appetizers. They were cheap frozen ones you find in a cheap grocery store. We totally overpaid for not good food.*
>
> *As far as the employees, they acted like we bothered them when we asked questions and ordered. My boyfriend simply asked a delivery girl a question and she rudely dismissed him like she was bothered. No one was welcoming.*
>
> *This place was not good. Maybe if you want something better than frozen.*[1]

Debbie's response, which comes from "Debbie G. Business Owner of Fresh Brothers Pizza," reads:

> *Hi Ray—I'm really sorry that you had this experience when you visited in March. We've made some changes in the store and I think the environment has really changed for the better. Would you consider trying us again? I'd like to send you a gift certificate so you can try us, on us! If you'd like to take me up on my offer, please send me an email with your mailing address and I'll send it out. Thank you. Debbie@ FreshBrothers.com* [2]

Perfect. She acknowledges the issues, apologizes, and provides a remedy. We'll evaluate how to respond to haters by channel in depth in chapters 6 and 7, but Debbie's reply here is a good template.

You may be thinking that this customer could just have been trying to scam Debbie out of a free meal, especially since it's obvious when looking at her replies on Yelp that she frequently offers gift certificates to unhappy patrons. We'll look at the dynamics and wisdom of that approach in chapter 5.

Regardless of whether she should be supplying hater aid in the form of gift certificates, the fact that Debbie is even publicly acknowledging and replying to complaints is unusual and commendable. As she says, "With the negative reviews, people still don't expect a response. Businesses haven't really caught on to the fact that you should be responding because we can, in a lot of cases, easily get these people back into a store, and hopefully get them to try our food again and rectify the situation."

One of the interesting elements of the Yelp platform is that it allows business owners like Debbie (or store managers, if she chose to delegate the task) to respond privately to Yelp reviewers. This is similar to Facebook's Messenger feature and Twitter's Direct Messages tool, all of which make public customer interactions behave more like private e-mail exchanges. (There are a lot of new and nuanced developments happening in this particular area, and we'll explore them in chapters 4 and 8). But Debbie rarely responds privately, even to haters, despite the fact that the technology to do so is at the ready. Why?

"The Yelp staff recommends that you contact complainers directly and not do it in a public way, which I think is really interesting and backward," Debbie observes. "To me, it just makes sense to do it publicly because I assume a Yelp review is actually a representation of the thoughts of many customers. So if they're commenting, then it's probably not just that one person who may have had that experience. So knowing that they're a one-voice representation of potentially many others, I think it is important to respond publicly."

Debbie also understands the spectator-sport nature of customer service, and that the onlookers are as important to satisfy as the haters. As she says, "Overall, I want people to know that, good or bad, we're listening and we care, and we're working on it. And we're the kind of people who are going to work really hard to get you back, to get you to come back and try us, on us."

A particularly unusual component of Fresh Brothers' approach to customer service is that Debbie also takes time to acknowledge and reward positive comments, not just negative feedback.

Here, Chris V. from Redondo Beach, California, publishes a five-star review for Fresh Brothers, with these comments:

> *Always GREAT pizza! The sauce is fantastic! Plenty of choices and for those who eat gluten free and/or vegan you can have great options as well! You will not be disappointed.*[3]

To which Debbie replies:

> *Hi Chris! Thank you for your kind words about Fresh Brothers. I'm so glad you enjoy the food. Please send me your mailing address so I can send you a thank you from the Fresh Family. All my best—Debbie@FreshBrothers.com*[4]

Fresh Brothers' approach to hugging their haters is a terrific example for small- and medium-sized regional businesses. But large, global companies can (and are) embracing customer service as a competitive advantage as well.

How KLM Royal Dutch Airlines Hugs Their Haters

If there is one company in the world that epitomizes the philosophy and lessons of *Hug Your Haters,* it's KLM, the official national airline of the Netherlands.

Compared to airlines in the United States, KLM's home market is quite small, with a population of approximately 16 million people living in the country. Consequently, KLM's primary business model is to transport as many people as possible from one part of the world to another part of the world. A major reason KLM has been able to succeed in that endeavor is that they differentiate their brand with customer service.

According to Karlijn Vogel-Meijer, global director of social media at KLM, "We believe that service is the basis of everything we do on social media, and that providing excellent customer service, that is the basis of everything we do."

In social media alone (not counting telephone and e-mail support), as of this writing, KLM has 150 employees answering questions and addressing complaints twenty-four hours a day, seven days a week, in fourteen languages. They are hugging haters in Dutch, of course, and also in English, Japanese, German, and even Turkish. They leave no interaction unanswered, and even provide a response time estimate at the top of their Facebook and Twitter pages, updated every five minutes. So if you want to ask a question of KLM, or sound off to them on Twitter, a quick glance at twitter.com/klm shows that you can expect a response within thirty-three minutes (at the exact moment I wrote this sentence).

How's that for accountability and setting expectations for customers?

But KLM's journey to being a fully formed customer service powerhouse was triggered not by a strategic planning session or executive decree but by a volcano.

In 2010, a massive eruption of the Eyjafjallajökull volcano in Iceland caused the cancellation of 107,000 flights over an eight-day period, impacting the travel plans of approximately 10 million passengers.[5]

As Vogel-Meijer recalls, it was chaos at KLM. "We had thousands of our customers trying to reach us, all at once. Obviously, back then, they first turned to e-mail, and phone. But then they turned to social media. We had a social media presence at the time, just like a lot of other brands, but we were just trying to figure out what to do with Facebook, and with Twitter. We just posted some nice stuff and that was mainly it. Suddenly, there was a flood of questions coming in from people asking us, 'I need to go to my wedding. How do I get to my wedding? I'm not able to get out of the Netherlands. I'm not able to get out of wherever.'"

One decision changed the short-term nature of how KLM dealt with their volcano-impacted customers, and this decision ultimately altered the corporate culture and fundamental DNA of the company. Vogel-Meijer remembers it clearly: "There was this specific moment where an employee went into the office of our vice president of e-commerce at the time and said, 'Listen, we can either pretend the questions are not there or we can start answering. But be aware, if we start, there won't be any way back.' And our vice president said, 'Answer them all.'"

Because planes were grounded, many KLM team members were sitting around the airline's home base at Schiphol airport in Amsterdam, with little to do but talk about airborne ash. So once the decision was made to engage every customer and answer every question and complaint, it was an all-hands-on-deck scenario.

"There were hundreds of people from all over KLM at tables with their laptops, answering questions from customers, and that was the start of our social media service program," Vogel-Meijer recalls.

KLM didn't stop responding to their customers once this particular crisis ended. Rather, they've just codified and expanded their service. And how could they stop, even if they wanted to do so? You can't very well say to your customers, "Yeah, that amazing customer

service we provided on Facebook and Twitter? That was just a volcano special!"

They never stopped, and neither will you. Because once you start
hugging your haters and embracing complaints, you'll never want to
let them go.

Answering every complaint and question, in every channel, every
time, requires substantial effort and commitment. But there is a
significant—and often transformative—business case for this
method, beyond just the psychically satisfying notion of answering
complaints because "it's the right thing to do."

Why Hugging Your Haters Makes Business Sense

Your business improves in four ways when you hug your haters: you
turn bad news good; you create customer advocacy; you gather
insights and intelligence; and you differentiate from your competition. How much each of the four benefits will impact you varies
based on the type and size of your organization.

Benefit 1: Turning Bad News Good

At its core, the most important reason to answer complaints and hug
your haters is that it at least gives you a chance to recover and retain
an unhappy customer. Too many businesses care too little about
retention, placing much emphasis on outbound marketing and the
attraction of new customers, with comparatively little attention paid
to keeping the customers they've already paid to get.

You may have heard the saying "Advertising is a tax paid for being
unremarkable." It's usually credited to Robert Stephens, the founder
of the computer and electronics repair company Geek Squad (now
part of Best Buy). A better and more accurate phrasing of that concept

might be "Advertising is a tax paid when you're poor at retaining your current customers," and you can attribute that one to me.[6]

As Janelle Barlow and Claus Moller wrote in their excellent book, *A Complaint Is a Gift:* "Many companies do not appreciate the real cost of losing customers. They can tell you exactly what they are doing to attract new customers and how much this costs them, but they may not have a clue as to how many customers they are losing, why they are being lost, or how much this costs them."[7]

This is remarkably shortsighted considering a 5 percent increase in customer retention can boost profits by 25 to 85 percent.[8]

One of the benefits of having complainers is that they can be discovered and found. You don't have to hunt for them, or wonder whether you are targeting the right audiences or market segments or fret about buying ads on the optimal radio stations. They just raise their hands via phone, e-mail, social media, and beyond. Haters step into the light on their own, which makes interacting with and, hopefully, recovering them a straightforward exercise, compared with customer acquisition.

Hugging your haters gives you the chance to turn lemons into lemonade, morph bad news into good, and keep the customers you already have.

Dave Kerpen understands this dynamic, which is why he personally responds to every one-star review of his books on Amazon. He apologizes and offers to refund money spent, plus money for the pain and suffering of having read the book. He's had three people take him up on this offer, and he sent each of them a check. Many others have commented that they were impressed by the response, but didn't feel right taking Dave's money. Beyond that, the impact of Dave's actions is powerful, because people reading reviews before purchasing a book see these exchanges in that crucial consideration period.

"There are many people who write on Amazon, 'Wow, I can't believe this guy did it. I'm definitely buying his book,'" says Kerpen. "It really works. Not because you're trying to trick people, but because you can demonstrate your authentic personality and show that you care."

The same offer holds for this book. If you leave a negative review of *Hug Your Haters* I'll find it and offer to refund your money.

This is in stark contrast to how British author Richard Brittain handled a highly critical, one-star review on Amazon of his book *The World Rose*. Brittain tracked down teenage reviewer Paige Rolland, traveled five hundred miles, and smashed her in the head with a wine bottle at the supermarket where she works, knocking her unconscious.[9]

You certainly shouldn't "mug your haters," and the unexpected largesse exemplified by Kerpen (and definitely not Brittain)—even in the face of great negativity—is a shock to the system, believes Debbie Goldberg from Fresh Brothers Pizza. "It's the art of misdirection. Throwing a compliment at somebody in the middle of negativity turns the situation around, and brings the power back to you."

That power can save a customer. Similar to the impact Dave Kerpen has had on his one-star reviewers, Debbie's habit of sending gift certificates to unhappy patrons can completely change the attitude of a customer who would otherwise defect. "We get e-mails from people that say things like, 'Thank you so much for the gift certificate you sent. My food was late and you made it up to me, and now we're back,'" she says. "It happens all the time, and we know it works."

Chapters 6 and 7 include step-by-step processes for handling haters, organized by complaint channel, but regardless of circumstance or complaint type, the most important element in customer recovery is acknowledgment of the mistake, according to Scott Wise from Scotty's Brewhouse. "You can take some of the worst complaints and most unpleasant experiences, and you can make those people into your most raving fans if you handle it properly. And that just means acknowledging them, acknowledging you've made a mistake, apologizing profusely, and making it right."

San Diego immigration attorney Jacob Sapochnick embraces a similar philosophy. In 2014, a client was extremely unhappy about how her initial inquiry was handled when she called the law offices, and subsequently left a pointed one-star review on Yelp. Sapochnick was alerted of the complaint by Yext (a software tool that organizes reviews) and immediately called the client, offering his services, normally priced at forty-five hundred dollars, at no charge. Fiercely protective of his previously spotless five-star average rating, Sapochnick never thought twice about making the expensive offer to try to recover the customer. She remained a client, and promptly wrote a very positive addendum to the initial review.[10]

Not everyone can or should offer free products or services to unhappy customers, but the financial outcomes of doing so are often far more attractive than you might imagine.

For large businesses, the number of incoming complaints and questions may be daunting (more about hater volume in chapter 5), but you can listen and respond to all of your haters, if you choose to do so. In 2015, Andrew Turko wrote a long e-mail to Apple CEO Tim Cook, asking for clarification on several confusing elements of the planned launch of the ballyhooed Apple Watch. Unexpectedly, Turko received a personal telephone call from a member of the Apple executive team the following day, who had been asked to call him by Cook himself. This changed Turko's feelings about the launch considerably, and he posted his original e-mail and a summary of the telephone call on the popular MacRumors online forum. Apple's commitment to quickly answering complaints—even those sent to the chief executive—was widely applauded by forum participants.[11]

We've seen how answering complaints can retain unhappy customers. But advanced practitioners of hater hugging can not only erase negativity but also convince previously irate patrons to spend extra time helping your business.

Erin Pepper is the director of marketing and guest relations at Le Pain Quotidien, a chain of bakery-cafés with more than 220 locations around the world. Erin reads every review and comment about every location, e-mailing them to individual store managers when relevant and necessary. (She uses software from NewBrand to help organize this process.) Erin and the Le Pain Quotidien team are adept at finding kernels of insight inside customer reviews, but her program of turning haters into advocates is so brilliantly simple and effective that people who hear the idea often say, "Why didn't I think of that?" When Erin encounters very negative reviews on Yelp or similar sites, she apologizes and tries to recover the customer in the same way Scott Wise suggests, by acknowledging the problem publicly and owning it. But then Erin takes hugging your haters up a notch.

She says (typically through a private message) something along these lines: "You know, sir, you are a discerning patron. You noticed deficiencies in our business that, frankly, most customers never see. What we'd like to do with your permission, sir, is digitally load funds onto a LPQ gift card. And what we'd like you to do is, anytime you'd like, please go to a different Le Pain Quotidien location near you. After your visit, I would ask you to complete a short online survey, and send me an e-mail detailing your observations about how we're doing, because you see things other people don't."

This is so smart. This tactic turns hate into help, creating a nearly free volunteer customer experience department comprised of previously disappointed and vocal customers.

Benefit 2: Creating Customer Advocacy

The comprehensive consumer study I conducted for this book with Edison Research found that answering customer complaints increases customer advocacy, regardless of complaint channel or type. Conversely, not answering customer complaints decreases customer advocacy across the board. But what does that really mean, and why does it matter? It means that not only can you recover a customer, but hugging your haters can enhance short- and long-term affinity for your business, create expressions of public support, and yield real financial impacts along the way. In spawning positive word of mouth, a successful service recovery can have twenty times the impact of regular advertising.[12]

It is a remarkable psychological phenomenon. When people have a problem and that problem is solved, they love you for it. It's the business version of the axiom "The best measure of a man isn't when things are going well, but rather when things are going poorly."

This dynamic—the ability to actually create customer advocacy using complaints and problems as a springboard—has been documented for decades. In his book, *The Squeaky Wheel*, Guy Winch, PhD, recounts how in 1978, John Goodman and his fledgling company, the Technical Assistance Research Program (TARP), was tapped by the RAND Corporation to oversee studies on customer service in the U.S. government.[13]

This and a second set of studies found that when complaints are handled to our satisfaction, we actually become more loyal than we were before we had the problem.

That loyalty produces not just happy, talkative customers but real revenue. You probably believe in your heart that customer satisfaction matters, but it matters in your wallet as well. Remarkable research from the Bain & Company management consulting firm found that in the U.S banking industry, customer advocates are each worth ninety-five hundred dollars more than detractors.[14]

And this impact isn't solely limited to restaurant patrons and retail banking customers. Spiceworks is a large website where software and hardware companies interact with their customers through ratings, reviews, and robust discussion forums. Tabrez Syed, vice president of community products for Spiceworks, says that businesses that consistently interact and answer questions and complaints create vocal fans. "When you've historically done a good job of showing up and being part of the community, your advocates will show up for you," he says.

Syed provides an example of how advocates speak out on behalf of companies participating in this business-to-business (B2B) platform. "There might be a question in the Spiceworks community about Unitrends [an enterprise data backup company]. Somebody will come and ask a question and then one of the people in the community who sees it might write, 'I've just pinged Katie from Unitrends. She'll be here to answer the question. I think they're a great product. This is how I use them.' If you have a good reputation, especially if the person who represents your company on Spiceworks has a good reputation, advocates will show up and often correspond on your behalf." The human and personal nature of how smart companies participate in Spiceworks is important, and is covered in depth in chapters 4 and 6.

One of the best-known examples of a business using customer service to create advocates is Zappos, the apparel retailer now owned by Amazon. Zappos is legendary for its commitment to customer experience, especially when consumers call the company with a question or problem.

Steve Curtin, customer service expert and author of *Delight Your Customers,* describes it this way: "Look at Tony Hsieh, Zappos's founder, who's quoted as saying, 'We don't look at customer service as an expense, we look at it as an extension of our marketing budget. We've created this legion of promoters, which saves us dollars in terms of having to market to people because we just let our delighted customers do it for us.'"

To get that economic benefit for your business, however, you have to first solve the customer's underlying problem or at least his concerns. Only then will you see the financial boost of turning that hater into an advocate, which will accrue over time. This two-step process is subscribed to by Rahul Sachdev, founder of Get Satisfaction, a customer service community platform company now owned by Sprinklr. Sachdev says, "At Get Satisfaction, we actually believe that complaints and problems are a huge opportunity for brands to connect with those customers and market to them. But first, you've got to solve their problems before you can go and say, "Hey, buy more stuff from me." Before that, you've got to make them happy, because unhappy customers don't want to buy from you."

Especially in today's hyperconnected, social media–fueled world, that process of making the customer happy and then successfully creating an economic impact can occur with breathtaking speed.

Discover Financial Services participated in a remarkable exchange on their Twitter feed in March 2013 that epitomizes this nimbleness.

Rob Speciale (@RobSpeciale) from Austin, Texas, sent a tweet that read:

> *Haven't checked my mail in a few days, and there are 3 offers for the @Discover card. Persistence, or lack of coordination?*[15]

Within nine minutes, Discover responded with a tweet of its own:

> *@RobSpeciale We must be excited to have you apply! DM w/ your full name & full address if you would like the mailings to stop.*Amy*[16]

Just four more minutes passed before Speciale replied with the following:

> *@Discover kudos for the prompt response time! Ok, I'll bite, mostly because of your response Amy. #Greatservice*[17]

In thirteen minutes flat, and with one well-timed tweet, Discover turned a hater into a new customer.

Response time matters when you're answering customer complaints, and the research conducted for this book shows that consumers' expectations of how quickly businesses should respond are growing, especially in social media. Even for individuals and micro-businesses, a near-instantaneous reaction can win the day.

In 2009, Peter Shankman, author of *Zombie Loyalists,* consultant, and then-owner of Help a Reporter Out (HARO), held a conference call for about seven hundred people, each of whom was paying fifty dollars to listen. The subject was how best to pitch the media, and speakers included reporters from the *Wall Street Journal, New York Times,* and *Los Angeles Times.* The call experienced massive technical difficulties, with ten scratchy minutes of conversation followed by fifty minutes of static. Attendees were understandably irate, and immediately took to social media to express their displeasure.

Shankman knew he had a responsibility to make the situation right—and that he had a narrow window of opportunity to satisfy his customers. Within minutes, he posted this statement to his blog, and distributed a link to it to attendees via e-mail and Twitter:

RESPONSE FROM PETER SHANKMAN AND HARO REGARDING TODAY'S CONFERENCE CALL

First things first:

Today's HARO "How to Pitch Business Reporters" will be rescheduled for tomorrow, Thursday, February 19th at 2pm EST.

Now then:

To my esteemed panelists, and to all the audience members listening in: I'm truly sorry. While the problem was caused by technical issues, the fact is, I organized the call, I promoted it, my panel convened at my request, and the audience paid for it on my recommendation. As such, I accept full responsibility for today's SNAFU, regardless of what caused it.

We don't know exactly what happened. What I do know is that I've used Conference Call University for our previous two calls, without any problems at all. We've never had so much as a blip of trouble on either of the previous calls, and had no reason to expect any different. Obviously, that's not what happened today.

I truly apologize to each and every one of you, and I vow to make this right.

Tomorrow's conference call will take place at 2pm EST, just like today's did. CCU will be responsible for giving out the conference call dial-in number for the audience members. For the panel members, I will call each of you personally an hour before the call and give you the dial-in numbers.

> *One final time: I'm truly sorry. For those who can't make the call tomorrow, I will personally send you an mp3 audio file of the call the second it finishes saving.*
>
> *Thank you all for your understanding. If I can answer any further questions, you know I'm available to you via email peter@shankman.com, via twitter @petershankman, or via a cup of coffee if we're in the same city.*
> —*Peter Shankman*

Within two minutes, comments starting appearing on the blog and on Twitter, and almost all of them were positive, such as:

> *Thank you, Peter. This is a stellar example of how to react when everything hits the fan, even when it was clearly beyond your control. I continue to have the utmost respect for you and am looking forward to trying the call again tomorrow!*
> *Best,*
> *Kary*[18]

Benefit 3: Gathering Insights and Intelligence

Answering customer complaints can recover customers and cause them to rush to your defense and actually spend more money with you over time. But one of the least-discussed benefits of hugging your haters and paying attention to customer feedback is the potential to glean insights about your business that can improve your operations and processes. After all, very few people complain without a reason to do so. Are you listening—*really* listening—to each of them?

It's important to recognize that haters actually take time to let you know what they think, giving you an opportunity to take action that not only could potentially mollify them but also could fix the underlying cause of the problem, eliminating complaints from the next batch of customers. Haters are the canaries in the coal mine. They are the early warning detection system for your business.

Remember, haters are not the problem. . . . Ignoring them is.

The real problem for your business is the people who have a poor experience but are not passionate enough about you and your company to take the time to say something about it in a form or fashion that you can find and act upon. They are the "meh" in the middle, and they are what kills businesses.

Renowned digital marketer, technology investor, and author of *Jab, Jab, Jab, Right Hook,* Gary Vaynerchuk has a blustery style that draws complaints from people who do not like his approach. But that's the group to which he pays the most attention historically. "I'm a big fan of people who are publicly negative about you, because the 'invisible negative' crew is the thing I'm most scared about," he says.

Dan Gingiss, formerly of Discover, concurs. "I would say don't be afraid of complaints. The fact that your customer is taking time out of their day to give you feedback means that they care. That should be appreciated. If somebody didn't care, then they would not necessarily feel the need to complain. They just go to your competitor."

I love the way Richard Binhammer looks at this dynamic. Binhammer is a business consultant and adviser who helped lead Dell's foray into social media customer service. He says, "Think about when you unfriend someone on Facebook. You don't reach out to tell them, 'Hey, screwball, I'm unfriending you because you're an idiot.' People just go and unfriend people. If they really care they'll call you out and talk about it before they give up on you. Customer service is the last call before you lose them. So don't assume just because they said they hate you that they actually hate you. They are telling you that they're upset with you and they do still kind of love you, otherwise they wouldn't be taking the time to ask for help."

Despite being sometimes painful to address, complaints and haters are very much the mathematical minority, increasing their value to your business. Indeed, the "meh" in the middle that doesn't care enough to log a complaint is a much, much larger group of dissatisfied customers. This has always been the case.

John Goodman's research at TARP on behalf of RAND began in the 1970s. In addition to discovering the customer advocacy impact of hugging your haters discussed above, he also found that 95 percent of disgruntled customers never complain to the entity responsible for their dissatisfaction.[19]

That 5 percent of your unhappy customers who do care enough to complain give you a road map for how to fix whatever ails your business. Because while the people who take the time to complain are a small percentage of your overall customer base, the conditions of their dissatisfaction apply to all customers. In this way, the haters are the vocal representatives of everyone your company serves.

"Last summer, we had an instance where we were getting a lot of complaints about our lemonade. People were saying that it tasted different than the year before, and that it was tart and sour. We noticed these complaints, and went back to our chefs, and they actually realized that the recipe wasn't being batched correctly in many locations. So they fixed it, and after that, we didn't receive any more complaints," recalls Erin Pepper from Le Pain Quotidien.

It was the handful of haters who took the time to complain that enabled Erin to find the problem and fix it. This fix then benefited not just the haters themselves but the silent majority who didn't like the lemonade but remained silent.

When you're able to analyze and act to improve your operations, complaints become not something annoying that have to be "dealt with" but rather massively valuable, free information that can be a catalyst for excellence. Rather than trying to reduce the number of complaints and eliminate haters, you should instead encourage complaints and make customer feedback mechanisms as plentiful and simple as possible.

The operations improvements that are bred in the petri dish of negativity also create other business benefits that impact the bottom line. This service multiplier effect can be massive in large companies that understand the relationship between complaints, insight gleaning, customer service, and subsequent customer experience tweaks.

Frank Eliason understands how this works, and has captained these programs for very large companies that attract a high volume of customer feedback, including the television and Internet access company Comcast, and Citi, where he served as the global director of the customer experience team. Eliason is also the author of the excellent book @ *Your Service.*

"The best dollars and cents come when you start to make process improvements based on feedback. It's harder to do with calls, and easier to analyze online. You can start to understand where your frustration points are and fix those. Each of those has a monetary value to them," he says.

Kristen Kavalier, vice president of customer relations at New-Brand, the software tool employed by Le Pain Quotidien to find, analyze, sift, sort, and respond to customers across many online platforms, explains how this works: "To a certain extent we'll report on star ratings and rankings and averages, but mostly we throw them away in our analysis and actually look at the content itself. What was the actual verbatim commentary and how can we break that down, categorize it, and score it in a way that we can create structure and meaning and intelligence from it? How can we can aggregate it all, and provide our customer with something really actionable? We want to create some intelligence from all the noise that's out there."

Square Cow Movers is a small, family-owned moving company based in central Texas with four locations. They handle long-distance and commercial moves, but the company's core service is local residential moves, according to managing partner Wade Lombard.

As a small operator, haters hit Lombard hard. The tendency is to take complaints personally because he and his immediate family are so intertwined in the business. It's their life and their livelihood. Lombard compares the emotional ties he has to his business to what he feels about his children. "I can go to my son's baseball game, and he can hit a home run, and I will feel like, man, that is my DNA, that is my offspring, I'm the best dad ever," he says. "And the very next day—this hasn't happened but it could—I can get a call from the principal who says, 'Hey, your son's in the office for disciplinary reasons,' and I'm so disappointed in whatever action he took to land there. And it's similar with business. One day I can feel so proud of what we've been able to build and what we've been able to do. And the next day, one of our guys can do something silly, or a client can call and they can have a legitimate complaint. And I will be so down in the dumps, my emotional spectrum will just plummet. And so I think for responding to complaints the key is to try to take the emotion out of it and say to yourself, 'What can I learn from this?'"

There are lots of details in the moving business, and much back-and-forth with customers, who are already on edge due to the stresses inherent in any move. Square Cow Movers wasn't handling those communication details well, a fact Lombard discovered by paying attention to complaints.

"What we found in the reviews was that most of the issues people had with us were when people were unaware of what time we were going to get there, or they were unaware of certain rules or regulations related to moving. And so what we started to do is pick up on patterns. We found these patterns of misunderstandings, and said to ourselves, 'Okay, because this is a pattern, obviously we're not doing our part to communicate properly,'" he says.

Lombard and his team changed company policy and procedure as a result, adopting a policy known as "Overcommunication is a myth." Today, the company goes out of its way to inform and educate customers multiple times throughout the moving process, and negative feedback based on misunderstandings has subsequently plummeted.

Benefit 4: Differentiate from Your Competition

So few companies hug their haters today that those that make this commitment are almost automatically differentiated and noteworthy when compared to their competitors.

Customer service and customer experience matter. And they're going to matter even more in the future. The world is inextricably linked now, by transportation and technology that was unthinkable twenty years ago. This global interconnectivity mutes the advantages of price and location that businesses formerly used to create market inefficiencies and gain a disproportionate share of customers.

There are more than a dozen banks in Bloomington, Indiana, the modest-sized college town where I live. All of them offer almost precisely the same core services, at fees that are not appreciably different from one another. From the perspectives of product and price, they are nearly indistinguishable. There are even more pizza places nearby, and they all offer roughly the same thing at the same cost, partially because they are buying ingredients at the same price from the same global suppliers, and are tapping into the same labor pool, where what you pay a college student to make pizzas is essentially the same for each restaurant. Likewise, my accountant and your accountant and my barber and your barber are doing almost the exact same things for approximately the same fees.

In today's world, meaningful differences between businesses are rarely rooted in price or product, but instead in customer experience. How does each provider make you feel when you interact with them? It is in the provision of standout, noticeable customer experience (the real-world embodiment of the brand promise) where great companies shine and mediocre companies shrink.

Why do I always order from the same pizza place in Bloomington? Because I live on the outskirts of town, and they cheerfully deliver to my house. Most of the other pizza places give me the terse "outside our service territory" story and refuse to bring me pizza.

The winning companies of tomorrow will be those that make

their customers feel the best, even if those customers are paying more for the privilege. This isn't just a circumstance that's true in consumer products, travel, and hospitality either.

The customer intelligence consultancy Walker released a research report that stated that in business-to-business scenarios, customer experience will be more important than price by 2020.[20]

"The B-to-B companies that will win are beginning to prepare now by recognizing the shift that's taking place, aligning the right resources, and focusing on the right metrics. Enlightened companies must view the customer experience as a strategic initiative. And, in the future, the responsibility of a 'chief customer champion' will become more common, serving one purpose—to create an unrelenting focus on the customer," states the report.[21]

John DiJulius, a well-known customer service consultant and adviser and author of *The Customer Service Revolution,* describes this differentiating factor as "outloving your competition." As he writes in his book, "'Outlove your competition' is one of my favorite sayings. Think about it. Nearly everything can be copied: the products or services that you sell, your decor, website functionality, menu, and prices. Can you really outwork your competition? Outthink them? Maybe not, but the one way you can get a distinct competitive advantage is by outloving the businesses you compete against. The only way to do that is to stop the typical squawking that goes on about how difficult customers can be, and just start appreciating them."[22]

Realize, however, that to truly differentiate your business with customer experience, you have to clearly outpace your competition in this regard. Making a commitment to "be better at customer service" isn't going to get the job done. Instead, as Walker suggests, you need to "create an unrelenting focus on the customer." There are many elements of a comprehensive customer experience program, and discussing all of them falls outside the scope of this book. But the first step in differentiating your business with customer experience should be to be demonstrably better than each of your competitors in how you embrace complaints. Start there, and if you can successfully hug your haters, you'll be on your way to a full-scale customer experience advantage that can literally be the difference between your business's flourishing in five years, when price and location are no longer deciding factors, and not existing at all.

Companies like KLM, Fresh Brothers Pizza, Le Pain Quotidien, Discover, and many more you'll meet in these pages are committed to not just answering the phone or replying to tweets, but rather to fundamentally refining the customer experience and customer service expectations in their category of business. And you can make the same commitment. Visit HugYourHaters.com to learn more about workshops, training, webinars, and participating in the Hug Your Haters community.

As Dan Gingiss says, "We firmly believe that customer service is the new marketing. Discover put its flag down on customer service since it started in the eighties. Discover was the first credit card company with 24/7 service. It pays attention to service and it's good at it. It talks about it on TV—the last two main television campaigns have been about service. And to me a complaint online is an opportunity for us to show off amazing customer service in a public setting that can't be done on TV and can't be done in any other channel. If somebody is having an issue with their product or their card that I know can be fixed, to me it's an opportunity."

Chapter 2

The Two Types of Haters and the DNA of Complaints

Complaints come in multiple formats, in many channels of communication, and in degrees of intensity. The haters who lob those complaints toward businesses aren't homogeneous either. In our research, Edison and I discovered that there are two main types of haters. These two groups of haters differ demographically in the frequency of their complaints, in their use and embrace of technology, and in how and where they choose to complain.

Understanding the two types of haters, and the differences between them, will enable you to spot them in the wild, and to provide the support and succor each requires. Knowing your haters gives you a much better chance of being able to tap into the four benefits of hugging them, because handling a hater incorrectly is almost as bad as not handling him at all.

Offstage Haters

The first group is offstage haters. The reason we named this segment of complainers offstage haters is that they almost always complain first in a private, one-to-one format, often by telephone or e-mail. Offstage haters are also slightly older, less mobile and social media savvy, and they complain somewhat less frequently on an annual basis.

Characteristics of Offstage Haters

Offstage Haters Complain in Private

91%
25- to 34-year-olds who have complained offstage

92%
Use social media

95%
55- to 64-year-olds who have complained offstage

2.84 offstage complaints per year (mean)

75%
Own a smartphone

Edison Research and Jay Baer, 2015

Complaints from offstage haters are often less strident and outlandish than many of the public complaints in social media and review websites. This is particularly true of e-mail complaints.

Julie Hopkins, digital marketing analyst at Gartner, Inc., has a theory as to why that's the case. "If you send an e-mail, you're pausing yourself to a certain extent. By choosing to complain via e-mail you put a requirement on yourself of crafting a message. You've basically said, 'I'm calm enough that I'm going to put together some kind of a reasoned argument in the hope that I'll receive a reasoned reply back.'"

Hopkins also believes that the "savable" nature of e-mail contributes to its comparative lack of rancor. "Even though we all know that social media is public, people recognize that e-mail is savable and is documentable. People are more aware that an e-mail is real, and able to haunt you down the line. So I think there's potentially a slight bit of additional care and concern that comes with sending an e-mail to customer service compared to other channels."

Telephone complaints come with a different set of circumstances. Because they are synchronous in a way that no other hater outlet is (even the best social media customer service teams take a few minutes to respond), the opportunity to unleash your wrath on the living embodiment of your ire is difficult to resist.

I'm not a big complainer personally, and typically fall into the dangerous "meh" middle category of disaffected consumers. But of the times I've cared enough to complain, I've been truly angry only when on the telephone. I'll wager the same is true for you.

You're already being forced (or feel like you're being forced) to take your time to complain. Then perhaps you've been stewing on hold for a while. Next, the person who is assigned to assist you doesn't understand the situation, can't easily access the information needed to address the issue, lacks empathy, or doesn't take any responsibility for his or her employer's shortcomings. You're being "helped" but not being heard. It just throws fuel on the fire and ratchets up the tension until you sound off on the customer service representative in a loud and dramatic performance reminiscent of a pro-wrestling promotion. Afterward, you feel bad. (At least I do. I'm not a sociopath.) But you also feel so, so good, even though the satisfying physical conclusion of an angry call is absent from today's smartphones. (Someone should invent a storefront business where you go to call customer service. The entire place could be rows and rows of old push-button and rotary phones, giving you, trembling with aggrieved frustration, the nearly extinct sensation of slamming a real handset into its cradle).

I'm not sure whether stewing on hold simmers you down when you're on the phone waiting for a company representative or gives you time to think through exactly what you're going to say, like pausing in the wings before you take the stage. Either way, it's perhaps not surprising that our tolerance for hold times is diminishing in this world of instant gratification. Research from Parature in 2014 found that 50 percent of people calling a company are willing to wait on hold for five or fewer minutes, and just 25 percent of people will wait for more than ten minutes.[1]

Even without the hold time, the satisfaction that accompanies getting a complaint off your chest by shouting it into a telephone is palpable even when you're just leaving a voice mail. There's something about vocalizing your complaints that brings out the id in each of us. This voice mail left for the Jimmy Dean sausage company is a particularly fine example:

> *This is Randy Taylor. I don't know where you people come from. I don't know if you test your products, your quality of your products. Your products are very delicious. I've loved your sausage for thirtysomething years, but I can't take and feed a family of five on a little twelve-ounce roll of sausage. I don't mind paying you more money for your sixteen-ounce roll of sausage, but you don't have it anymore. You've got a twelve-ounce roll, and you've got three men that weigh over two hundred pounds apiece, a woman that's a little plump Scotch girl, and a daughter who is thirteen, and you're going to try to take a twelve-ounce roll of sausage and a couple of dozen eggs and feed that? It ain't going to work, and I'm not going to purchase your product anymore or ever again. And as far as your sixteen-ounce maple and sage sausage? I don't eat that. I'm not from the North. I'm a Texas man. Jimmy Dean sausage is for Southern people to eat with their breakfast, with their fried eggs and their T-bone steaks. And I can't feed a twelve-ounce package to four, five, six people. And I'm not going to buy two of those twelve-ounce packages just because you want to downsize and charge the same [bleeping] price. I'd sure like a reply. . . .[2]*

Let's hear it for Randy Taylor, a man with a serious sausage problem!

Onstage Haters

The second group of complainers is onstage haters. We named them onstage haters because they almost always complain first in a public venue—social media, review sites, discussion boards, or forums. Compared to offstage haters, this group is slightly younger, certainly more mobile, with more technology and social media savvy. Onstage haters also tend to complain more often, partially because they can do so from their smartphones in a matter of seconds.

Characteristics of Onstage Haters

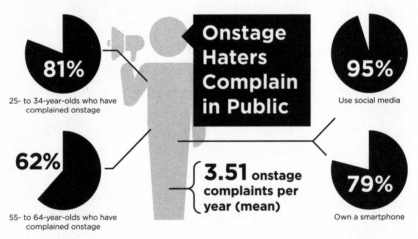

81% 25- to 34-year-olds who have complained onstage

62% 55- to 64-year-olds who have complained onstage

Onstage Haters Complain in Public

3.51 onstage complaints per year (mean)

95% Use social media

79% Own a smartphone

Edison Research and Jay Baer, 2015

Today, for most businesses, offstage haters are still the majority, and most customer complaints are made in a private format. Our research found that 62 percent of complaints are first made via telephone or e-mail. But the balance of power between offstage and onstage haters is shifting rapidly due to ease of use and perceived differences in outcomes.

Procedurally, it can be far faster for customers to complain in social media and through mobile applications like Yelp, TripAdvisor, and even dedicated complaint apps that we'll investigate in chapter 8. These near-instant complaint channels also allow the customer to voice a complaint with a business before she's even left the premises. Taking the time to sit down and craft an e-mail requires gratification delay and additional time and effort.

Telephone is viewed as even more of a hassle, according to a 2014 study from Lithium and Harris Poll:[3] "Who wants to call a customer service center to resolve a technical problem, product defect, or billing error? Fewer and fewer people, it seems. In fact, a vast majority of adults surveyed will only dial a toll-free number for support as the absolute last resort. Around two-thirds of American, British, and Australian adults and nearly three-quarters of French adults feel this way. The only outliers are German adults, with only 46 percent resisting the urge to pick up the phone. What's not surprising, however, is how these numbers vary by age group—with younger people, regardless of country, consistently less likely to pick up the phone compared to adults 55 and older. But the data are starting to tell a compelling story about the future of customer service that is quickly shifting away from the phone in favor of digital communications."[4]

Dan Gingiss is already seeing this shift toward online complaints. He suspects that in addition to smartphone technology, companies are getting better and faster at providing service in social media, thus training their customers to become onstage haters: "Over the last year or so Discover started to see a shift. It definitely used to be that social was a channel of last resort. Now, for those people that use social as a customer service channel, they're seeing they get faster responses. They don't have to pick up the telephone, and it's generally an enjoyable experience. I've actually seen a shift toward social becoming a channel of first resort."

This move away from private complaints and toward public complaints is revolutionizing the very nature of customer service, and has massive implications for staffing, technology, response times, customer expectations, and satisfaction levels. The rise of the onstage hater changes everything.

"You know it would be nice if people would just let me know privately when we screw up, but that's not the world we live in now," laments Scott Wise from Scotty's Brewhouse.

Comparing Offstage and Onstage Haters

There are no meaningful differences in educational level or annual income between hater types. There are also no gender differences of note between onstage and offstage haters. However, men complain more often across all channels combined. In our research we asked respondents how many times they complained to a company or business in the prior twelve months. We found that 19 percent of participants fall into the "heavy complainers" category, defined as having made seven or more complaints to businesses in the past year. Twenty-two percent of men complained to a business seven times or more in the past year, compared to 16 percent of women.

Age has a significant impact on how and where people complain. More than 90 percent of American complainers, in nearly every age category, have complained offstage via phone or e-mail in their lives. Even in eighteen- to twenty-four-year-olds, a group that came of age surrounded by alternatives to the telephone, nearly 82 percent have complained offstage.

With regard to onstage haters, however, young people are far more likely to have complained via social media, discussion boards,

Offstage and Onstage Complaints by Age

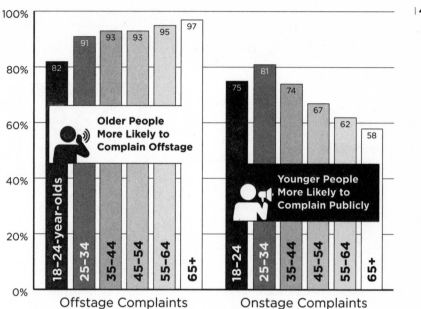

Edison Research and Jay Baer, 2015

forums, and online review sites than older consumers. More than 80 percent of twenty-five- to thirty-four-year-olds have complained publicly, compared to 58 percent of survey respondents aged sixty-five or older.

Because smartphones are so pervasive among American adults, and because people can be (and usually are) both onstage and off-stage haters at some point, there is not a major difference in smart-phone ownership among offstage and onstage haters. Onstage haters are approximately 5 percent more likely to own a smartphone than offstage haters.

But the most remarkable effect of smartphone and social media usage is on overall complaint volume and likelihood of complaint: 84 percent of frequent complainers own smartphones, compared to 67 percent among occasional complainers.

Smartphone Ownership Rates by Complaint Frequency

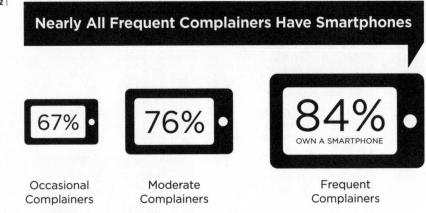

Nearly All Frequent Complainers Have Smartphones

67%

76%

84%
OWN A SMARTPHONE

Occasional
Complainers

Moderate
Complainers

Frequent
Complainers

Edison Research and Jay Baer, 2015

As we'll discuss in the next chapter, Facebook is a favorite haven for onstage haters. But when examining the relationship between channels and complaints, I begin to wonder whether Facebook's pervasiveness, ease of use, and "look at me" ethos is disproportionately fueling onstage haters. After all, you have to create status updates about something, and "I've been wronged by this company" is a good way to solicit interactions from friends and digital acquaintances.

Of frequent complainers, 94 percent have a Facebook account, and among research participants who claim to use Facebook several times per day, nearly one-quarter of them have complained seven or more times in the past year. That group of hard-core Facebook fans is 300 percent more likely to be frequent complainers than people who do not use Facebook at all.

Although the total number of users is smaller, this dynamic is even more pronounced with Twitter. While 70 percent of heavy complainers have a Twitter account, nearly one-third of the respondents who use Twitter several times per day are frequent complainers. Across every social media platform including Facebook, Twitter,

Facebook Usage Among Frequent Complainers

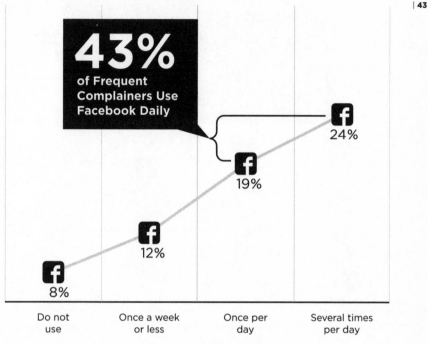

Edison Research and Jay Baer, 2015

Pinterest, Instagram, Snapchat, Vine, WhatsApp, and WeChat, the heavier the usage, the more likely the consumer is to complain about businesses. Given the proliferation of social media and social networks, this isn't going to change anytime soon, if ever. Social media facilitates complaints by reducing the interpersonal friction and time necessary to do so.

Do They Want an Answer or an Audience?

But are these really complaints, in the classic sense? The issues that are communicated in social media, review websites, discussion

Facebook and Twitter Usage Among Frequent Complainers

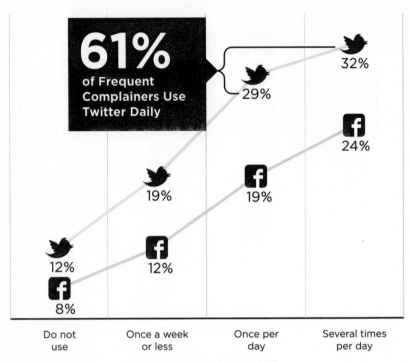

61%
of Frequent
Complainers Use
Twitter Daily

32%

29%

24%

19%   19%

12%   12%

8%

| Do not | Once a week | Once per | Several times |
| use | or less | day | per day |

Edison Research and Jay Baer, 2015

boards, and online forums can be more frivolous than those in telephone or e-mail interactions. Especially in social media, consumers
often post quick missives without much depth.

Mason Nelder, director of Central Insights and Social Business at
Verizon, sees this difference every day: "Typically, the people who
send e-mail have, I think, much more meaning behind what they're
writing, because it's long form. In social media, because it's short
form, it's much more emotional. It's almost like, if they took time to
think about it and actually write about it appropriately, it might not
be as emotionally charged."

What we categorize as a complaint in social media (in particular)
may not be a complaint in the same sense that a well-crafted e-mail
or a telephone call is a complaint. Instead, these short, social missives

are often simply expressions of the current situation. And among heavy social media users, any customer experience falling short of perfect is legitimate grounds to instantly admonish the business. In the same way that bumper stickers are the most shallow form of political expression, social media grousing is the thinnest form of customer complaints.

Offstage haters want an answer. In many cases, onstage haters want an audience.

When people complain in private they almost always expect a response from the business or company. Yet when complaining in public, onstage haters expect a response roughly half the time or less. This ratio varies by channel, and we'll explore those differences in depth in the next chapter.

Richard Binhammer saw this difference during his time at Dell. "Often, even when customers are being difficult in public, they're just calling you out to get your attention. And once they've got your attention they actually turn around and can become good customers."

This distinction is also evident in other countries. A survey of two thousand online complaints in the Netherlands in 2013 by TNS found that 30 percent were venting negative feelings, and 23 percent were seeking vengeance. Only 48 percent wanted help.[5]

My friend from high school and college Alan Moir is disproportionately concerned about beverage temperature. He is fond of saying, without irony, that "there's no such thing as too much ice." This is perhaps an unexpected thing to obsess over for a Canadian, since the "drinks must be as cold as possible" notion is a primarily American construct. Yet a person like Alan can quite easily use social media to proclaim, "Hey, Le Pain Quotidien! How about some more ice in the lemonade," while still drinking that same lukewarm beverage. He can express his displeasure in an instant, at no personal cost. He may even be able to interact with the brand (which can be a bit of thrill), or, at the very least, put it out there for his friends in social media to react to alongside him.

Guy Winch explains why we do this in his book *The Squeaky Wheel:*

> *When we complain, we hope to purge the frustration, anger, or irritation that is generated by our dissatisfaction. Indeed, the expression* getting it off our chest *refers to the palpable lightness, the cathartic easing of internal tension, we hope to experience by speaking up about a troubling complaint. But what creates the catharsis is not the voicing of our complaints aloud, but rather voicing them to* another person.[6]

It's much easier to get it off our chest online than it is offline. Would Alan take the time to telephone about the ice issue? Would he sit down at a computer and write out an entire e-mail? No. The platform used to voice the complaint usually fits the nature of the crime against the consumer. The bigger the issue, the more likely it is that contact will be through private, offstage channels. This is true of the first complaint only. If an issue requires more than one contact to solve satisfactorily, a much different scenario can occur.

Even though the tragedy of a beverage-specific ice shortage isn't cause for a move to DEFCON 4, the business in question still has to deal with it, because it's now in the public domain. And if you don't answer that complaint, it not only reduces the customer advocacy of the complainer, anyone looking on might be frustrated and disappointed in your lack of attention as well. Remember, customer service is now a spectator sport.

A lot of what we call complaints when delivered online and in public would be classified as comments if delivered offline. Annoyances that formerly would have qualified for an inner monologue of "Oh, that sucks" now spur an "Oh, that sucks and I should share it with the world."

But to garner the attention they desire (from companies, their friends, and the public at large), onstage haters often have to up their rhetorical game, to stand out amid the same messaging clutter that companies have to face when trying to market their wares (a scenario for which I provided an antidote in my book *Youtility*).

"The complainers? They have to break through the noise as well," says Mason Nelder.

This is why many onstage haters' complaints are delivered in an outlandish and overwrought fashion, way out of proportion to the seriousness of the issue. On first contact, we rightsize our channel (smaller problems are registered with onstage complaints), but we do not rightsize how we describe our angst.

I implore you to spend five or forty-five glorious minutes watching the YouTube channel of a production company called Gotta Kid to Feed. The channel is titled "Real Actors Read Yelp Reviews," and it's a hilarious collection of twenty-three (and counting) short videos. They illustrate precisely what I mean about onstage haters employing amazing rhetorical flourishes to get noticed. Find it at YouTube.com/user/gottakidtofeed.

This transcribed example of a two-star review for Carnival Cruise Line does the video—and actress Thérèse Plummer—almost no justice, but gives you a sense for the outlandishness of onstage haters' complaints:

> *A floating cafeteria with gaudy decor, loaded with screaming children running wild. While their parents, with apparently no parenting skills, dine and party the night away with the false sense of security that, just because they're on a boat, none of the thirty-one-hundred-plus people would ever dare hurt, molest, or toss overboard (which crossed my mind), their bratty, little nose pickers. Never, ever again.*[7]

To stand out, onstage haters sometimes go beyond inflammatory language and ensure they have an audience by buying it. In 2013,

Hasan Syed's father flew British Airways to Paris, and his luggage was lost. Syed went to the British Airways Twitter account to complain, but found that the account was not monitored during the evenings. Frustrated, Syed spent more than one thousand dollars to buy advertising on Twitter, delivering a tirade of anti–British Airways tweets to hundreds of thousands of users. He specifically targeted followers of the British Airways Twitter account with "Thanks for ruining my EU business trip #britishairways. I shouldn't have flown @BritishAirways. Never flying with you again."[8]

Despite the scope and scale of this rancor, British Airways replied with:

> *Sorry for the delay in responding, our Twitter feed is open 0900-1700 GMT. Please DM your baggage ref and we'll look into this.*[9]

Haters aren't the problem. . . . Ignoring them is. British Airways has flights around the clock. Yet their customer service is open ten hours per day, at least on Twitter. Without this gap, would Syed have purchased ads? Of course not.

British Airways could have answered his initial tweet in fifteen minutes, even at night. But that's not how their customer service program works. KLM would have answered Syed because their program is set up to do so.

In situations like these—and many others—hugging your haters can be a competitive differentiator.

When Haters Become Crazies

It's difficult to ascertain why or how haters looking to stand out cross over from pointed (and often colorful) criticism to something more frightening and dangerous, but it happens, and it's often not really related to their problems with your business.

"When people are really lashing out, in any type of situation, it's about projection. It's an unconscious defense where something within that human being is unhappy, and you end up projecting that out into the world," says Dr. Marcy Cole, a holistic psychotherapist based in Los Angeles. "There's a big difference between healthy, legitimate frustration and rageful projection, which is a situation where it becomes expanded, inflated, and inappropriately expressed and shared."

Even though it's a statistical rarity, when you think about the challenges of hugging your haters, you think about this "rageful projection," don't you? Every person I interviewed for this book at some point talked about dealing with the third type of hater . . . the crazies. These are the customers who cannot be satisfied or mollified, regardless of how and when you interact with them. They are the trolls of the Internet.

There are at least three different methods of dealing with the unhinged haters: ignoring them, researching them, and hugging them.

Wade Lombard at Square Cow Movers believes in ignoring the crazies, at least in terms of public, onstage interactions: "One rule we have is we don't do crazy; 99.8 percent of our clients are the kindest, most level-headed people in the world, but you are going to get crazies sometimes. And once a person crosses over the threshold of crazy, and is beyond reason, we just say, 'Hey, you know what? In the future we're just going to go ahead and correspond in writing. If you'd like to e-mail us, that's fine. We'll e-mail you back, but we feel like we need to archive everything going forward.'"

Note that Lombard refuses to answer crazies in public, but he does answer them—each of them, at least in private. That's the only way he can determine whether someone is a regular hater or an off-the-rails customer.

Century 21, a large real estate company with offices across the

United States, pursues the avenue of researching first, then acting based on what it finds. Matt Gentile, global director of social media, explains, "If the conversation online takes a turn that is unacceptable and beyond the pale, we'll do the research into the person. We'll try to find out a little bit about them and understand what they are saying on their own Facebook pages and Twitter. Are we dealing with somebody who's kind of a serial complainer? Is it something where there's not a lot of validity in terms of the complaint right out of the gate? If you can see that they've made complaints to fifty other brands in the past thirty days, well, that's a good indication that you can probably prioritize that person in a different manner."

Those patterns of behavior can be quite telling, and research into how to identify and classify Internet trolls aims to help keep the Web free of hate speech and other inappropriate and destructive commentary. Researchers from Stanford and Cornell universities analyzed 40 million online comments across a variety of websites that solicit strong opinions and devised an algorithm that successfully predicts with 80 percent accuracy whether or not a person will eventually be banned by the community, solely based on the content of his first five comments.[10]

Twitter is also putting in place new technology that will identify and suppress hate speech, an issue serious enough that the company's then-CEO cited it as a major barrier to the platform's continued growth.[11]

The team at Microsoft Xbox has no need for these tools to find and delete posts from over-the-line haters, because they hug them all, regardless of circumstance. Microsoft Xbox set the Guinness World Record for the most responsive brand on Twitter, and James Degnan, the community support manager for the channel, says they don't try to determine which customers to respond to; they just respond to them all.[12]

"People are smart. They realize, 'Hey you're going to address this guy because he's easier to address. But you're not addressing me. I can see you're picking and choosing.'" And Degnan says that the angriest haters can still be hugged: "The louder or more upset the customer is, the more of an opportunity it becomes to turn them around."

The best way to keep your customers is to understand them, and in the next chapter we'll dive into the Hatrix, the full analysis of who complains where, and what they *really* want when doing so.

Chapter 3

The Hatrix: Who Complains, Where, and Why

Businesses that answer every complaint, in every channel, every time are businesses that consistently exceed customer expectations. They create advocacy gains that translate into real revenue.

You have to hug haters across more platforms. This is especially true in the onstage venues where companies often refuse to participate.

Edison Research and I asked more than two thousand individuals who had complained to a business in the prior twelve months whether they expected a response when they complained, and if they did expect a response, how quickly they anticipated the business to reply.

Our findings form the basis of the Hatrix: the expectation and corresponding advocacy impact for onstage and offstage haters. (A poster of the Hatrix is available within these pages, and it is free and downloadable at HugYourHaters.com as well. Take a moment to grab it now, and keep the Hatrix in your office to remind you of these key points.)

Do haters expect a response?

Just as onstage and offstage haters differ in their use of technology, they also diverge in their expectations of a response. When customers complain in a direct, offstage manner such as by telephone or e-mail, they anticipate that businesses will reply. Specifically, when complaints are made by telephone, customers expect a response 91 percent of the time. E-mail expectations are virtually identical; 89 percent of complainers who use that channel as their first contact mechanism anticipate a reply.

| 53 |

Among respondents, 84 percent of phone complainers and 78 percent of e-mail complainers actually received a response.

The expectations for response among onstage haters is far different, however. When complaining in social media, customers expect a response just 42 percent of the time, and 40 percent receive one.

When complaining on a review site like Yelp, TripAdvisor,

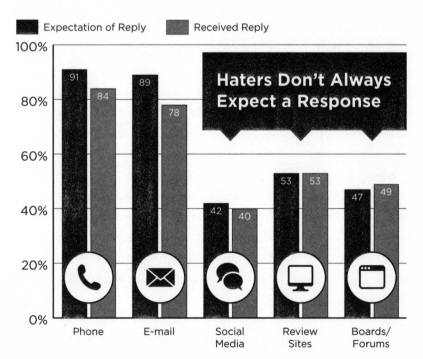

Percentage of Complainers Who Expect a Response Versus Complainers Receiving a Response, by Channel of Complaint

■ Expectation of Reply ■ Received Reply

Haters Don't Always Expect a Response

	Phone	E-mail	Social Media	Review Sites	Boards/Forums
Expectation of Reply	91	89	42	53	47
Received Reply	84	78	40	53	49

Edison Research and Jay Baer, 2015

Amazon, or similar online venues, 53 percent of those onstage haters expect businesses to reply, and 53 percent of the time a reply is received.

In discussion boards and forums, 47 percent of complainers expect a reply, and their complaints are addressed 49 percent of the time.

Businesses must manage expectations better.

Remarkably, the legacy, offstage channels are where companies are failing to meet the desires of today's customers. How much goodwill is being squandered with the 11 percent gap between expectation and reality in the e-mail channel?

The chart above shows the significant differences between offstage haters who want a reply and an answer and onstage haters who often want an audience and don't even expect a reply half the time.

How Fast Do Haters Expect a Response?

When I first designed this study with Edison Research, I anticipated a far different set of findings. I fully expected to discover that in today's hyperspeed world, speed of response would have the greatest impact on customer advocacy; that being fast would be the currency of satisfaction. But it's not entirely true, at least not yet. Speed of response has an impact on overall customer satisfaction and the willingness of haters to embrace your business postcomplaint. But the impact isn't massive yet. This is partially because when complaints are addressed, companies are doing a satisfactory job at answering them without delay. The problem is that many complaints are never answered.

If you want to retain customers with great customer service and customer experience, it's not just about being fast, it's about being everywhere.

Of haters who complain by telephone, 67 percent are satisfied with response time, and 75 percent of today's telephone complaints are handled by businesses within twenty-four hours.

E-mail doesn't fare as well, with 61 percent of haters satisfied with response time on that channel. This is perhaps because just 52 percent of e-mail complaints are addressed within twenty-four hours.

Onstage haters' expectations for a speedy response are quite different. Just 32 percent of social media complainers are happy with how fast businesses respond in that channel. This is despite the fact that 63 percent of social media complaints that are addressed are handled within twenty-four hours. That's not fast enough.

Today, 39 percent of social media complainers who expect a reply want it to come within sixty minutes, yet the average response time from businesses is five hours. Closing that expectation gap is a major element of the Hug Your Haters success formula.

Haters who complain on Twitter are the most satisfied with response time: 88 percent of complainers who receive a reply there are happy with the speed of that reply. This may be because many businesses in the United States and around the world have come to view Twitter as a primary customer service vehicle, and have assigned significant resources to the channel.

But according to our study, this Twitter-centric model of social media customer service may be misplaced. Of all social media complaints in the United States, 71 percent are logged on Facebook, with Twitter a distant second at 17 percent. Google Plus represents 6 percent of complaints, and Instagram another 5 percent.

Certainly, Facebook has far more users than Twitter, which may partially explain the volume of complaints there. But many customers also take to Facebook to sound off in ways that may not be directly actionable or solvable. Often, Facebook complaints are structured, negative feedback more than they are cries for specific help. These are viewed as complaints by consumers, but may not be viewed as such by businesses. This discrepancy may cause companies to misjudge the scope and scale of customer service opportunities. They

U.S. Social Media Complaints, by Social Platform

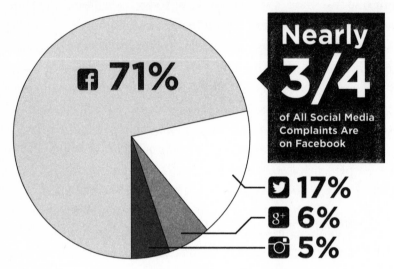

Edison Research and Jay Baer, 2015

seem to favor Twitter, where the overall participation may be lower, but the use of the venue as a direct customer service channel is more obvious.

Your ability to find indirect complaints (negative comments about your business that do not explicitly tag you and are not written on an online site you control) varies by platform. On Facebook, for example, privacy controls selected by the consumer dictate how much indirect commentary a company can see and find, making software almost a requirement for companies serious about online customer service. Trying to find indirect complaints unassisted by technology almost ensures you'll miss important opportunities to answer them, which can have a massive impact on advocacy.

Dan Gingiss recognizes Facebook as a customer service venue, saying, "There are still many brands that don't let you post on their Facebook walls. Discover does. That obviously invites more commentary and complaints, but don't be afraid of it. If you don't let people post to your Facebook directly, then you are left with people inserting their comments into your marketing posts, which may cause the discussion to derail from what you wanted the original marketing piece to be about. I have held fast to the belief that customers should be allowed to write on the Facebook wall."

Since the pace and cadence of interaction on review sites are not as quick as they are on Facebook and Twitter, haters' expectations for response times on these sites are not as aggressive, and their over-all satisfaction is higher. About half of the people complaining on a review site are happy with response times from businesses, and 62 percent of the replies received there occur within twenty-four hours.

The speed dynamic is similar for discussion boards and forums,

Percentage of Responses Received Within 24 Hours, and Haters' Satisfaction with Response Time, by Channel of Complaint

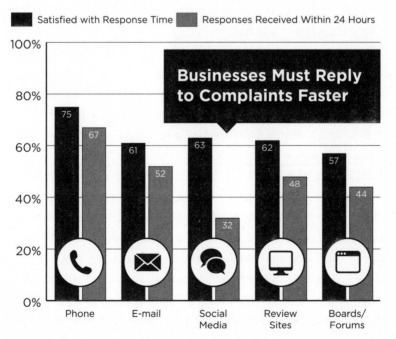

Edison Research and Jay Baer, 2015

where 44 percent of haters using those venues are satisfied with response times, and 57 percent of replies are received within one day. It is important to recognize here, of course, that most onstage complaints are never addressed at all.

How Much Does a Reply Matter?

Answering complaints increases customer advocacy. Not answering complaints decreases customer advocacy. This is true for all haters and across all complaint venues. But the greatest advocacy impact occurs when you hug your haters who don't expect you to respond— the onstage channels, as shown in the chart above. Customers have come to anticipate a particular style and speed of response from businesses. If you can defy or exceed those expectations, it creates a "shock and awe" effect, making customers far more likely to advocate on the company's behalf.

We asked consumers to rate how likely they would be to recommend the business they complained about to a friend or colleague on a ten-point scale. This is similar to the Net Promoter Score methodology first developed in 2003 by Satmetrix, Bain & Company, and Fred Reichheld,[1] now often used as a standard for evaluating customer experience and advocacy.

We asked customers how likely they were to recommend the business at the time of their first complaint. Then we asked them how likely they were to recommend the business after their complaint was addressed (or not addressed). The difference, or "lift," between these two votes of confidence in the business comprises our advocacy impact data for *Hug Your Haters*.

Before complaining, haters using the telephone averaged 5.8 out of 10 when asked how likely they would be to recommend the company to a friend or colleague. Among those who received a response, their average score on likelihood to recommend was 6.4 after

Percentage Increase (or Decrease) in Customer Advocacy if Hater Receives a Response to a Complaint, by Channel of Complaint

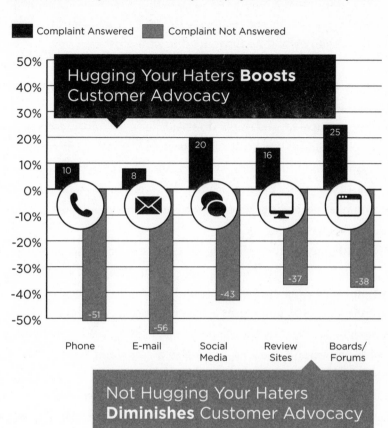

Edison Research and Jay Baer, 2015

receiving a reply from the business. This is an increase in advocacy of 10 percent.

This is a minor lift, but there's a very good reason for it to be so slight. Remember that when consumers complain on the telephone, 91 percent of them expect companies to respond. When your business does answer the phone or place a return call, it's quite difficult to exceed those expectations and trigger a significant advocacy impact. This is the same dilemma faced by utilities and monopolies worldwide. The act of successfully picking up garbage is nearly devoid of awe. Answering the telephone is the customer service equivalent of that type of utilitarian interaction. It is simply expected at this point.

Conversely, because consumers anticipate that their telephone calls to companies will be responded to in almost every case, when that doesn't happen, the negative impact on advocacy can be massive. In fact, not responding to a telephone complaint reduces customer advocacy an average of 51 percent.

This low upside and high downside is even more evident for e-mail complaints. Successfully answering an e-mail complaint increases customer advocacy by 8 percent. However, not answering an e-mail is grounds for a customer divorce. Haters who complain over e-mail experience a huge 56 percent decline in advocacy if their e-mail is not answered.

With offstage haters, there is minimal advocacy upside to hugging them, but considerable downside to not doing so. With onstage haters, however, the upside of responding is much higher.

Responding to a complaint anywhere in social media has double the impact of answering the telephone, generating a 20 percent advocacy lift on average. Not responding to a complaint in social media decreases customer advocacy by 43 percent.

The results are roughly equivalent when businesses participate in review sites like Yelp, TripAdvisor, and Amazon. Customer advocacy increases 16 percent when complaints are addressed. When negative reviews are not addressed, as is often the case today, advocacy declines an average of 37 percent. It makes a bad situation worse. Further, one of the primary benefits of participating in review sites, of course, isn't just to increase advocacy among the original complainer, but to demonstrate to onlookers that your business cares.

We trust online reviews to a remarkable degree. According to 2015 research from BrightLocal—a local search engine optimization consultancy—80 percent of American consumers say they trust online reviews as much as personal recommendations in some circumstances, up from 67 percent in 2010.[2] This is not just an American phenomenon either. Reviews drive consideration and purchase in many parts of the world. Around three-quarters of British and French adults, and about two-thirds of German and Australian adults, say they will not buy something that doesn't have positive online reviews. This is amplified even more among young adults.[3]

If people believe in online reviews that much, why wouldn't your business participate in those venues as well?

The same is true for online discussion boards and forums: the original social media. Participation in discussion boards and forums creates more consumer advocacy than in any other channel of customer service. Answering customer complaints there boosts advocacy by an average of 25 percent, mostly because only 47 percent of haters expect a reply at all. Failing to respond to a complaint logged in a discussion board decreases advocacy by 38 percent, roughly on par with review sites and social media.

Companies sometimes choose to not participate in forums because they can feel like very niche places. It's very easy to dismiss a forum as a place where people go to debate and criticize, not to shop or seek customer service. But there is a big difference between the connections among friends that drive participation in Facebook and the connections by topic that power forum participation. The intensity of feeling in forums is significant, and far afield from the "weak ties" that are present in most mainstream social networks.

Ted Sindzinski is senior director of marketing at SVS, a manufacturer of audio components that is very active in discussion forums read by consumer audiophiles. He explains the difference between forums and more mainstream platforms using a personal example: "My friends on Facebook don't care that I'm a mountain climber. Most of my friends don't climb mountains. They like my photos, but they don't know what gear I should buy. So of course I'm going to go to forums for that. It's where the people that love what I love spend their time."

The upside of responding to onstage haters is far greater than responding to offstage haters, and the downside is somewhat lower. You of course still need to reply to complaints on the telephone and via e-mail, because they still represent the majority of overall complaints, and not doing so creates negative impacts of more than 50 percent. But in terms of exceeding customer expectations and triggering positive customer advocacy, the biggest opportunity is in forums, review sites, and social media, a concept we'll investigate in more detail in the next chapter.

Chapter 4

Customer Service Is a Spectator Sport

When you address onstage complaints (or even acknowledge positive or neutral feedback) you have a chance to dramatically boost customer advocacy. That alone is a good reason to hug those social media, review site, and discussion board users.

It doesn't end with the one hater, though. Every onlooker is a potential customer.

As author and consultant Dave Kerpen says, "If a customer calls you on the phone to complain, surely you wouldn't hang up on them. And not responding in social media is akin to hanging up on them, only worse, because there are actually other people watching and listening."

Imagine that every time you called a business, a few dozen other customers were allowed to listen in on the call. Would customer service be different? The concept seems far-fetched, but that's precisely how public, online interactions in social media and other onstage venues are. Everything online is amplified. Your interaction with customers is amplified. If you choose to not interact, that silence is amplified, too.

"What's the value in responding to one person? It's the magnification. What's the value of opening the door for one lady when you're walking into a building? Well, to that one lady it means a whole lot. But it's also the other six people who might have seen you, who now may have a different perception of who you are as a human being. You cannot overvalue a good action, especially online where everyone is watching," says digital marketer and author Gary Vaynerchuk.

The Rise of Onstage Haters

These public venues, where everyone is watching how businesses react, may become the most popular way for customers to interact with companies. Onstage feedback may surpass offstage feedback when today's younger consumers become the dominant group of purchasers and possibly before then.

My children are fourteen and seventeen years old, and of course both have smartphones. But that's really a misnomer, because getting them to use the "phone" portion of that device is like enticing a ballerina to wear golf spikes. They abhor talking on the phone, and actively avoid it. They text . . . a lot. And they use apps constantly. They check e-mail only when looking for online purchase confirmations. They talk on the phone only at the point of a metaphorical bayonet. Imagine what will happen to legacy, offstage feedback mechanisms when their generation makes up the majority of your customers. I cannot believe that they will wake up one day in their twenties and think "Wow, I have really missed out on the wonders of telephonic interaction."

Even today, customer service practitioners and observers are seeing a rising tide of onstage questions, comments, and complaints.

Dan Gingiss sees this transition already. "In the millennial generation there just isn't much desire to pick up the phone and call an 800 number. They feel it's easier to tweet. I'm definitely seeing a shift."

E-mail may suffer the same decline, according to Scott Wise from Scotty's Brewhouse: "I don't think e-mail is going to be the be-all and end-all. Because people want instant answers. It's not just the millennials, and it's not just this younger generation, it's all of us. We are just becoming very ADHD from everything that we are surrounded with and all the stimulus that's being thrown at us at all times. Everything is at our fingertips and we feel like the minute we shoot off an e-mail, if we don't have an answer in five minutes, then someone is ignoring us." (See chapter 8 for more about Facebook's plan to take over e-mail.)

This shift from offstage to onstage is already in full swing for businesses with customers who tend to skew somewhat younger, like Microsoft Xbox. Xbox community support manager James Degnan reports that in the past five years, the number of interactions handled by his Twitter customer support team has increased tenfold.

Today's onstage complainers don't necessarily expect a response from you. But give them one dose of excellent customer service online and they're hooked. It's like the first time you listen to a supremely catchy song. You instantly want to hear it again. So one of the great paradoxes of today's customer service landscape is that the better you are at interacting with customers online, the more you are training your customers to expect that same treatment again and again.

As Dan Gingiss puts it, "There are so many brands that are not responding in social media that when you experience a brand that is, you realize that it's a fast, convenient way to get your question answered. If you tweet once and are impressed by the response, the next time you need service, you're going to be thinking about that channel first."

This phenomenon of good online interactions producing more desire for online interactions occurs worldwide. A poll of four thousand UK consumers found that two-thirds of those who have used social media for customer support now prefer it to traditional call centers.[1]

This raises some interesting questions about why companies are providing better and faster service online than they are offline. If your goal is to shift customer contact to online venues, perhaps this carrot-and-stick approach is warranted. But unless your objective is to reward and incentivize customers for complaining onstage, perhaps a better plan would be to provide the same quality of service across all venues. This is how Gingiss organized Discover's customer service department. The goals for response time and customer satisfaction are shared by all channels and do not vary based on whether they are online or offline.

You may be worried about this inexorable rise in onstage feedback and complaints. It is a lot to handle. But from an economics perspective, this shift can be a major win for businesses of all types and sizes.

Handling a customer interaction in social media costs less than one dollar, on average, compared to two and a half to five dollars for an e-mail interaction, and more than six dollars to provide telephone customer service.[2]

Every time a customer wants to interact with your business and selects an onstage channel instead of an offstage channel, the stakes are raised because the interaction is public. That's the challenge. But if you save five dollars every time a customer chooses to interact publicly, isn't it worth it to handle your business out in the open?

Today, however, the potential economic benefit provided by onstage interaction isn't being realized by most businesses because many of the onstage complaints are simply offshoots of an original offstage complaint. Yet what Discover, Xbox, and other brands are experiencing is that the number of customers choosing onstage channels first continues to increase steadily, especially when those consumers have had good experiences on those channels previously. But for now, many onstage haters are born first from poor offstage customer service.

When Offstage Haters Become Onstage Haters

Let's say you call or e-mail a company and are unhappy with the response time or the answer you receive. So you raise the stakes: you go public, and use an onstage channel like Twitter, Facebook, Yelp, TripAdvisor, Amazon, or a discussion board to make your ire known. You no longer want just an answer; now you want an audience. And magically, the company gets back to you right away and solves the problem it was seemingly unable to solve on the phone or through e-mail. This is a common scenario. Research in the Netherlands by TNS found that 71 percent of all online complaints occur because of failing traditional customer service.[3]

Yes, you can have a bigger impact on customer advocacy when you interact with onstage haters. And yes, the volume of public feedback will continue to increase because young people hate phones and e-mail, and you are training customers to use social media by being more responsive there than you are in offstage channels. But the biggest reason to hug your onstage haters is that in many cases, you have already disappointed them twice. They were disappointed first by whatever inadequacy or mistake caused them to complain. And now you've disappointed them a second time by not handling their call or e-mail in a form or fashion they deem acceptable. So you've got a twice-bitten customer using a public venue as a last resort, or to lash out. Still, many businesses choose to ignore these people.

Mason Nelder from Verizon says he and his team often encounter these frustrated onstage haters: "They've already tried by phone. They've already gone to the store. They've already sent an e-mail. And now they turn to social media or something like that as a last-ditch effort."

Onstage haters often have one foot out the door when they use public channels to blast your business. A response at this crucial juncture is your chance to turn things around.

One of the most difficult elements of modern customer service, however, is discerning whether a consumer is using an onstage channel after being genuinely mishandled in an offstage channel, or whether he just wasn't happy with the answer he received on the phone or in an e-mail. Is he aggrieved, or just trying to play Mom against Dad? For this reason, unifying online and offline customer service databases is critical. I'll cover that topic in detail in chapter 6.

Katy Keim is the chief marketing officer at Lithium, a software company that helps big brands find, organize, and respond to customer feedback. She describes the scenario this way: "One of the things I hear brands say is, 'Some of these customers are just using a public forum to get a different outcome than what they've already been told.' And it happens, in a case like, 'I've been told my TV is out of warranty, I've called the call center, I checked with the warranty desk, everyone has told me I'm really sorry, and then I get on Twitter and I'm like, I can't believe Manufacturer X won't honor my warranty, and I try to get a different outcome.' And so I think there's going to be a rightsizing of how complaining is dealt with. I think brands are struggling to figure out what's the productive response versus what they're being shamed into because it's a public forum."

Of course some customers will try to find inconsistencies in what they are being told in different venues, and will leverage the very public nature of onstage channels to extract a better deal for themselves. There will always be customers who try to work the system, and blaming social media or review sites for it is like shooting the messenger.

In high school, I worked at TG&Y as a stock boy and returns clerk. (TG&Y, now defunct, was in the 1980s one of America's largest chains of variety stores, with as many as nine hundred locations.) Once, when I was working the returns counter, a straight-faced customer arrived and announced that he wanted to return underwear. Upon inspection, I determined that this underwear had been worn. As a sixteen-year-old, this was an offstage customer interaction beyond my training, so I sought the counsel of my manager (whose name was Mr. Big, potentially the most appropriate name for a department store general manager in history), who informed me that we would accept the underwear in exchange for store credit.

The absurdity of the decision was plain to my linear teen brain, and I protested. But Mr. Big said it was better to keep the customer happy, and I begrudgingly provided fifteen dollars' worth of store credit. I'm not sure I agree with that decision even now, and perhaps you don't either. After all, hugging your haters doesn't mean the customer is right; it means the customer is answered.

But even if you think that customer was a cad and a bozo, you can't blame the car that brought him to the store. Yet businesses and businesspeople often blame social media or review sites for "allowing" customers to try to weasel a better deal, as if Facebook, by its very existence, were changing the value system and inherent honesty of customers.

Some of your customers suck. They sucked fifty years ago. They will suck fifty years from now. Technology doesn't change that and never has.

I believe that most customers do not suck. They are just trying to get a situation resolved, which is what Ray Lonis from Cabarete in the Dominican Republic was trying to do.

Jose O'Shay's is a sports bar and restaurant in Cabarete that caters to tourists and locals. Seeking to capitalize on expected big crowds and a must-see game between the New England Patriots and the Seattle Seahawks, the restaurant raised their prices 66 percent for the 2015 Super Bowl. This price increase wasn't posted, however, and that didn't sit well with longtime loyal customer Ray Lonis.

A former corrections officer in New York who relocated to the island, Ray watches NFL games at O'Shay's every other Sunday during the season, and is especially fond of the all-you-can-eat pig roast barbecue special on Sundays, usually offered for 450 DOP (approximately $10.00). On Super Bowl Sunday, when Ray went back for a second plate of barbecue, a waitress yelled at him, *"Solo un"* (just one). He protested to O'Shay's owner, Frank, who agreed to allow Ray another helping.

But when the bill arrived, the price was 750 DOP, instead of the usual 450. Ray asked if the price was right, and Frank said that it was. He wasn't charged for the second plate, but the price had increased. Ray argued that a price increase surely needed to be posted somewhere, in some fashion. To which Frank pointed out that the menu includes in minuscule type, "Restaurant reserves the right to change prices for special events."

Ray left full of pork but profoundly unhappy and suspicious. The next day, he went to an online community forum called "Everything Cabarete," where local issues are discussed, and said he didn't like the "surprise ending" he experienced at Jose O'Shay's. Several residents commented on his post that they had experienced similar circumstances, and that the price increase practice has been occurring for years.

"I wasn't happy about the way things went down," recalls Ray. "I put it out there to see if anyone else was in the same boat. If you go someplace and get bad service, you should post it so other people don't get ripped off. If enough people say something, it's probably true. If there's smoke, there's fire."

Frank from Jose O'Shay's ultimately did it right—he went on to hug his onstage haters and responded to the customer complaint in a venue that is most often overlooked by businesses: discussion boards and forums.

Hugging Haters on Discussion Boards and Forums

The best opportunity to grow your business with customer service is to engage with your onstage haters. And the best opportunity to engage with your onstage haters isn't in social media (yet).

The increase in customer advocacy that results from answering a customer complaint is greater on discussion boards than anywhere else. That may be because so few companies choose to engage in these channels.

Patrick O'Keefe is a discussion board expert and the author of *Managing Online Forums*. He believes all companies should be monitoring and participating in relevant forums. "I really encourage brands to participate in forums because it's where the most passionate customers hang out. . . . It's so powerful to go into forums and answer questions because becoming a part of the community helps the members of that community see you in a more favorable light. If the company is participating in the forum, and they offer a service and you eventually want that service, the company is going to be top of mind."

He acknowledges that many businesses choose to not answer questions and complaints in forums because they can be niche and insular. Success can also be more difficult to measure compared to other venues for customer interaction.

"Why I think a lot of companies are reluctant to participate is because it's harder to track," he says. "You don't own that community. You don't have access to the database. You don't have even the surface level analytics from Facebook that they provide you with. You don't really have a lot of information about direct results from within the forum. You can look at thread view counts [how many times the topic has been viewed on the forum] and you can look at how many people visited your website from the forum, but that's about it."

O'Keefe also reinforces that, like in all onstage venues, the audience on discussion boards and forums isn't just the customer providing feedback, but potentially all members of that online community. "I always tell people, when you respond in a forum, don't respond to the person who posted, respond to everyone who will ever read that conversation."

And that conversation could be read much, much later. Many online communities last for a long time, and they typically have high rankings in Google and other search engines, due to their topical authority and specificity. So if someone searches for your business name or the name of one of your products, a question asked three years ago in a forum might appear on the first page of search results. Isn't that a question you'd want to have answered?

Forums are often detailed repositories of information. As a result, they are most likely to be consulted when people are ready to make a purchase (and thus are using very specific search queries), or have already purchased (and have very specific questions about the product or service). Try it now. Set the book down for just a moment, and do some online searches for your company and your products. Links to forums may not be in the top ten results, but you'll find them eventually, and the more detailed the search term, the more likely forum posts are to appear.

Because of the nearly infinite digital shelf life of forums, the value of replying may persist indefinitely, but O'Keefe still recommends responding quickly, ideally within one week, with twenty-four- to forty-eight-hour response times a worthy objective.

Since discussion boards and forums are often true communities, with a core cadre of members participating with consistency, it is ideal if you can have the same person within your business—maybe even yourself—engage in a particular forum every time. This builds recognition and trust that can boost advocacy, and benefit of the doubt as well.

Esteban Kolsky is a social business strategist whose company, thinkJar, works with many large organizations on their social media customer care initiatives. He says that in the best forum programs, the participating persons become indispensable members of the community at large, due to their knowledge and accessibility.

"You need to put people in these forums who can answer the questions, your subject matter experts. You can build communities around those people, and have them solve as many customer problems as possible, in real time," Kolsky says.

Ted Sindzinski from SVS agrees: "Our forum participants are not people we hired off the street. They are people who are product experts. My marketing team is pretty sophisticated, but we don't make or support the product day to day. It's easier to train somebody in how forums work than it is to teach somebody everything about a product. I can't learn twenty years of audio experience as fast as someone could learn to post on a social network or an online community."

He says that forums aren't just part of the SVS customer service playbook but are integral to the business itself: "At SVS, forums and participating in them are core to the company's history. It's literally how the company grew when it was a small initial start-up. It was seeding product awareness in forums. It has always been part of the company's DNA, and even though many companies still don't participate in forums, for us, it's just a given. For every person who posts a question in a forum, you have five or ten or twenty more who find us. It's hard to find an exact number, but we get indicators all the time of how important the forums are to SVS."

Discussion boards and forums aren't just for consumer products either. In just about every industry and locale, there is an online community for a dedicated group of professionals, hobbyists, or potential customers looking to connect. In the United States, massive numbers of health care decisions are made—at least in part—by patients reading and participating in forums. There is a dedicated forum for nearly every disease, condition, malady, and remedy in existence. There's even a very large discussion board for plastic surgery. It's called RealSelf.

Every day on RealSelf, members post more than twelve hundred photos, either of themselves or of body parts they wish to emulate. And to date, the platform has accumulated more than a million comments and answers from plastic surgeons.

Tom Seery is the founder of RealSelf, and he explains its success this way: "These procedures are highly unfamiliar purchases. It can be very awkward. So our focus is on helping a physician become more relatable and relevant to the consumer who is looking for a physician that she can feel personally connected to before making a decision. We help that doctor answer consumers' questions, which allows him to demonstrate his expertise. And the doctor is able to also express his personality and showcase that his interests aren't just in making another credit card swipe of his patient, but that he also actually wants to help people make better decisions. We also provide a platform for patients to share their experiences. 'Was your tummy tuck worth it or not?' And as you dig into the site you can see people are not just writing reviews, they're really sharing journeys and telling stories."

Patients review physicians and specific procedures on RealSelf as well. Due to medical privacy regulations, most physicians do not answer reviews specifically in classic Hug Your Haters fashion, but instead participate indirectly by answering questions and providing assistance in the forums.

Discussion boards and forums are also important in the B2B economy. One of the largest of these is Spiceworks, a comprehensive online community for technology professionals that bills itself as "Where IT goes to work."

When B2B technology companies want to participate in the Spiceworks community, they nominate individual team members to do so. Spiceworks provides training materials on the best ways to interact with IT end users on the platform, and participants receive points and recognition based on their contributions. Once participants reach a threshold that indicates that they are trusted members of the Spiceworks community, they are given the label of Green Guy or Green Gal, marking them as official representatives of their company on the platform.

This personal touch matters, according to Spiceworks' executive director of marketing communication, Jen Slaski: "The more companies can make customers feel heard, the more they can explain something, the more people can see you're taking feedback and you're trying to make a difference, that goes a long way." She says that customer complaints change, and their overall ire diminishes when they realize they are talking to a real person, a representative of the company instead of "the company" as a faceless entity.

Priscilla Jones is one of the faces of HP on Spiceworks. Her official title is HP social media ambassador, and she represents the massive company in a large and important online venue. It's a busy job. As of this writing, she has written 1,986 posts on Spiceworks, and her contributions have been named "Best Answers" 124 times. She has also authored 106 replies tagged as "Helpful Posts" by the Spiceworks community. Priscilla is also a member of 65 groups within the platform, including the "virtualization" group, the "Oakland, California" group, the "motorcycle" group, and the "women in IT" group.[4]

One of her Best Answers on Spiceworks, and a good example of the potential impact of participating in forums, occurred when she answered a question about an HP printer from "ChrisJG."

He wrote:

> *Hi All,*
>
> *I have a P4515X printer that shows that it is a P4014n printer on the configuration page printout. It's never been used outside of trying to set it up and test. The person before I took over said he was having issues with the networking part of the printer, but he left this position before resolving the issue. I've updated the firmware to the latest, 04.221.6, on the HP website, but that didn't resolve anything (not that I really thought it would). I've tried resetting the printer to factory settings, and working with PJL files, but I can never get them to update the identity of the printer. I've read that in situations like this, you need a "multibyte file" from HP Support, but since this printer is no longer under warranty, I'm not sure I would be able to get a file. I would really appreciate any suggestions as I am completely stumped at this point. Thanks!*

Priscilla replied one hour and sixteen minutes later, including links to specific resources:

@ChrisJG, you may have noticed in your research of your issue that replacing parts, especially the formatter, can cause a printer to have "an identity issue." You may have also noticed this post in which @dicka confirms that the "multibyte file" has to be obtained from Tech Support and @dicka gives very detailed instructions on how to use the file. <u>Click here.</u> You will observe in this post that @dicka gives the names of staff to whom to send the information for the file. <u>Click here.</u> If this is old information, please call Tech Support at [phone number] to request the file. If you encounter problems please ping me. I see that this is your first post. Welcome to Spiceworks!

Chris responded:

Thanks for the info Priscilla. I did come across those linked posts and was able to create and send the PJL file to the printer to update the serial number and model number, but the problem still remains. I'll ping Tech Support Monday morning to see if they can assist. Will I still be able to get a file even though the printer is no longer under warranty? Thanks!

Priscilla answered:

Hello ChrisJG,
Thanks very much for the update. I felt that perhaps you had already seen those posts. Let me ping you regarding your Tech Support call. [Note that after this message, Priscilla contacted Chris in private, using the messaging function of Spiceworks.]

Chris then replied:

Thanks for all your help Priscilla. HP support came through with the multibyte file. My printer has been cured. Thanks!

And Priscilla wrapped it up beautifully:

> *Hello Chris, thanks very much for the positive update. Wonderful news! Your update has made my afternoon. Please let me know whenever your products need "curing." Enjoy the holiday break.*[5]

It's not difficult to provide great support in forums. But you do need to devote knowledgeable people to it, and give them the opportunity to make themselves human and approachable.

Hugging Haters on Review Sites

Review sites are the venues that businesses love, hate, and love to hate. A five-star review is a beautiful thing. A one-star review is decidedly less so. And reviews matter in every industry, which is why so many hyperspecific ratings and review platforms now exist. Thumbtack and Angie's List rate local contractors. Kitchen Cabinet Reviews specializes in exactly what it says. Goodreads is for books. DealerRater is for car sales. G2 Crowd is a platform for ratings and reviews of B2B software. And ApartmentRatings pretty much says it all in the name.

And the same way SVS built their business on forums, other businesses are building their customer bases through effective use of online reviews. In his book *Everyone's a Critic,* Bill Tancer chronicles the story of Hotel 41 in London. With 1,974 TripAdvisor reviews (1,778 of which have five stars), the property is rated by TripAdvisor as the number one hotel in the entire London area, outpacing more than one thousand other options.[6] This is, of course, by design.

Instead of spending money on ad campaigns, or discounting their room rates to appeal to big hotel-booking websites (Hotel 41 appears on none of them), the property instead invests in a level of service that spawns new five-star reviews, thus continuing the cycle and keeping them on top.

Onstage Complaints, by Complaint Venue or Platform

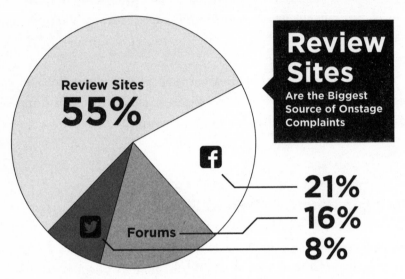

Edison Research and Jay Baer, 2015

Wrote "Douglas L" of Windermere, Florida, in his review of Hotel 41:

> *I'm really torn on providing my feedback on this hotel. My family and I just spent 4 nights at the "41". I consider it more of a private club than just a hotel. If everyone were to experience the level of service and genuine hospitality that my family did, then it would surely be everyone's top choice to stay while in London, and my ability to get future reservations will be severely diminished. If you want to stay at a large hotel where no one calls you by name, doesn't remember your favorite drink, and charges you for club access, then this is not the hotel for you. If exceptional personalized service is what you are looking for, then there is no better hotel in London. When in London this is where I will stay.[7]*

The key to the success of this program isn't just the great service; it's that the hotel staff knows where its bread is buttered. They care deeply about their TripAdvisor reviews and pay attention to them slavishly. As Tancer relays in his book, one of the hotel managers admits, "[We] all have TripAdvisor set as the home page on our smartphones. . . . We're constantly checking our ranking and looking for new reviews."[8]

Other businesses, of course, have a decidedly less cheery view of review sites. In what has become a meme in the independent eatery industry, several cafés in different American cities now have chalkboard signs on the sidewalk with some approximation of this message: "Come eat a pastrami sandwich that some guy on Yelp thinks is the worst in the world!"

Making light of a bad review may seem counterintuitive because we tend to remember negativity, but mathematically, the haters are outnumbered on review sites. Morgan Remmers is the manager of local business outreach at Yelp and says that 79 percent of the ratings on the platform are three-, four-, or five-star reviews. Certainly, three-star reviews often contain some element of complaint, which is why you should be reading all reviews left about your business in all venues.

One of the concerns businesses may have about participating in review sites is that some of the reviews may be erroneous, created by competitors, or otherwise not on the level. Indeed, "review farms" do exist, and these shady online professional services firms are paid to create an influx of seemingly legitimate positive reviews (or negative reviews attacking a competitor). Daniel Lemin's book *Manipurated* examines and exposes this industry, and certainly makes you look at reviews with a dose of suspicion.

For its part, Yelp says it is trying to fight back, and is taking legal action against review farms. In 2015, it sued three website operators who allegedly tout their ability to help business owners improve their reviews. Amazon filed a similar suit to fight fraudulent reviews.

"While Yelp's online reviews are a trusted resource for consumers to learn about local businesses, unfortunately some try to game the system and undermine that trust, by building businesses based on fraudulent reviews, invasive spam, and conduct that otherwise violates the law as well as Yelp's terms of service," Yelp alleges in its complaint.[9]

Yelp also says it has in-house technology to find and weed out fake reviews. PR specialist Hannah Cheesman says, "We have recommendation software in place which aims to highlight the most useful and reliable reviews out of the millions submitted to Yelp. So essentially what that's doing is it's trying to weed out the reviews that look spammy, or solicited, or have some kind of intrinsic bias."

Businesspeople who participate in Yelp say that this software has done an admirable job of eliminating many of the dodgy reviews. However, a common complaint is that Yelp simultaneously uses this system to reward businesses that pay to advertise on the platform at the expense of those that do not. This is a charge aggressively denied by the company, and they built a Web page to showcase their defense at http://www.yelp.com/advertiser_faq.

The B2B software review site G2 Crowd tackles the trust question differently, by requiring all participants to use their LinkedIn profiles when creating an account on the platform. As a result, all G2 Crowd raters and review writers use their real name, whereas Yelp, TripAdvisor, and most other consumer-based sites allow usernames or partial names, like "Susan G."

B2B companies participating in review sites are less common today than B2C participation on venues like Yelp and TripAdvisor. But G2 Crowd, Spiceworks, and other onstage channels very much encourage companies to get involved and answer customer questions and complaints. According to G2 Crowd president Tim Handorf, of the four thousand different software companies that have been reviewed on the site, approximately fifteen hundred have created an account and are participating in the forums.

"I believe they should respond when negative reviews are left on G2 Crowd about their software," Handorf says. "That's my personal belief. It lets the world know that you care about your customers. . . . Even though everything may not be perfect, you're trying your best to make things right."

The best possible way to engage with customers on any rating site is to answer every review. If it's positive, say thank you. If it's negative, apologize. If it's neutral, use the feedback to make your operations better, like Le Pain Quotidien or Fresh Brothers Pizza. But if you don't have the resources to answer every review, at least hug your haters and answer the negative ones. This doesn't have to be difficult, or particularly time consuming. Your response just needs to be empathetic, timely, and useful. Here's a relevant example on TripAdvisor for a Ramada Inn in Saskatoon, Saskatchewan, in Canada. The headline of this one-star review from user WanderingRoots is "Not good!" It reads:

> *Too bad there wasn't a ranking worse than terrible. If you plan to stay here, don't expect to sleep. There's a bar with noisy music that goes until 2 a.m. Noisy bar patrons and the hotel doesn't care. Front desk claims there was nothing they could do about the music roaring or the rowdy patrons screaming in the parking lot all night.*

That's a tough review to swallow, but a hotel manager answered quickly and hugged the hater. He wrote in his reply:

> *I would like to personally apologize for the series of unfortunate incidents that you experienced during your stay with us. We continually try to do our very best for all of our guests, but unfortunately, sometimes we do fail. I will look into each issue that you have noted, in an attempt to correct and improve our hotel policies. I would invite you to contact me personally at [phone number] to discuss this with you further or email me. Regards, Murray Waters, hotel manager.*[10]

While these local reviews and ratings can be the lifeblood of small businesses, they can also have an enormous impact on regional, national, and even global concerns, as their larger reputations are pegged to customer opinion at the local level.

"Think about businesses that operate hundreds or thousands of locations," says Jeff Rohrs, chief marketing officer at the reputation management software platform Yext. "Their brand reputation isn't just won at a national level; it's won store by store in the communities they serve. Even the most reputable brands see individual store sales flag in the face of bad local customer experiences. As a result, such brands need to train and empower local managers such that they can respond to negative online sentiment in a manner befitting a company that wants to be a lasting part of communities it serves."

Some businesses are taking response to reviews to another level and creating videos showcasing their answers. One of the first to do so was John Howie. In 2009, while chef and owner of the Seastar Restaurant and Raw Bar in Washington State, Howie filmed YouTube videos of his responses to negative customer reviews on Yelp.

An early video in the series included this message from the chef:

> *Hi, this is John Howie of the Seastar Restaurant. I'm going to respond to a few more reviews. Not all the reviews we're going to respond to are going to be positive, so let's have some fun here. Here's one, it's two stars. It's from Jane D in Seattle and it reads, "Crappy food, crappy service. I expected way better from experienced owners." I'm not sure what went wrong here, but I'd love to give Jane another chance to come into the restaurant, and if she'd be willing to contact me, I'd love to send her a gift certificate and maybe we can get her out and see if we can fix that experience for her.*[11]

This concept of answering your haters on video has become a hot trend. It was popularized by the American late-night talk show host and comedian Jimmy Kimmel, whose recurring "Celebrities Read

Mean Tweets" segment became a runaway social media sensation. Now similar ideas are popping up all over, even in government. Australian senator Sarah Hanson-Young regularly reads her own "mean tweets" via YouTube videos.[12]

Maybe hugging your haters on video robs the negativity of some of its power? Maybe poking fun at complaints makes it easier to not take them personally? Maybe you could video some of your own responses?

Should You Solicit Reviews?

Unless a majority of them are negative, having more reviews is better than having fewer reviews. Sometimes the total number of reviews for a product or company is prominently displayed on the website, and can serve as visual shorthand that helps consumers decide to click or purchase. This is the case on Amazon, where total number of reviews is shown in nearly all side-by-side product comparisons. Authors crave reviews, as they are rumored to influence how Amazon promotes books on the site and in their e-mails. Having more reviews also helps your business overcome occasional negative reviews because it keeps your average rating high.

It's good business to ask your customers to provide reviews, as long as it isn't too aggressive or a quid pro quo. I was on vacation in Lisbon, Portugal, and hours after concluding a walking tour of the city, I received an e-mail from the tour guide reminding me that TripAdvisor reviews are important to his business. No discounts were offered, nor threats for noncompliance. It was just a timely reminder, which is the way review solicitation should be handled. Speaking of which, I'd love it if you reviewed *Hug Your Haters*.

There's a fine line between encouraging reviews and demanding them. Even Yelp, which without a steady stream of new reviews would be as useful as a knife and fork in a hot-dog-eating contest, discourages businesses from overtly asking for reviews.

"We don't recommend businesses ask for reviews, mainly because they're more often than not logically only going to ask the people who look like they had a good experience. That could cause a bit of bias on our site. We recommend not asking for reviews but just encouraging engagement. Things like having links in your e-mail newsletters to your Yelp page, or including the Yelp logo on business cards . . . and posting signage on your reception table or window storefront," says Yelp's Morgan Remmers.

As a practical matter, however, businesses do often ask their customers to provide Yelp reviews, says Martin Shervington, who runs Plus Your Business, a local reviews consulting firm. "What we've found is that when there is a more personal connection between the business and the customer, whether it's a server, a manager, an owner, customers are more likely to provide a review," he says. "Trip-Advisor and Google do not prohibit or discourage review solicitation the same way Yelp does, but businesses everywhere are asking for reviews, and they should."

His point about Google is important, too. As Google continues to integrate consumer reviews of hotels, restaurants, attractions, and local businesses right into search engine results pages, a visit to a specific reviews website becomes superfluous in some instances. Google reviews are officially called the Google My Business program (formerly Google Local), and are highly influential due to the enormous reach of Google in search, mapping, and beyond. Will these ultimately become the most important reviews of all? I wouldn't bet against it.

Certainly, there is a line that shouldn't be crossed when it comes to demanding reviews. It can even be illegal to do so. In 2015, the United States Federal Trade Commission settled a case with Ameri-Freight, a Georgia-based vehicle shipper. The settlement required the company to stop using terms such as "highly rated" and "top ranked" in its advertising, as reported on the technology news website *Ars Technica*. The firm charged customers an extra fifty dollars if they did *not* write an online review of the service at transportrev iews.com, and removed the fifty-dollar charge if a review was written. Customers who wrote reviews were also entered into a "best monthly reviews" contest. Compensating customers for reviews without disclosing that information is a violation of the FTC's online marketing guidelines first released in 2009 and updated in 2013.[13] Other parts of the world have even more restrictions on these solicitations.

The best practice is to let customers know you participate in review sites, and that you care about their feedback, however and wherever they choose to provide it. That might require a verbal mention from a team member, signage, a follow-up e-mail, or some other interaction that makes the point plain. But charging customers who don't write you a review is half pushy, half stupid, and wholly illegal.

Should You Create Your Own Review Site?

Certainly, the proliferation of review sites means that there is probably one or more on the Internet that makes sense for your business. But in addition to those third-party venues, you may want to adopt a customer review system that you own and control.

Bazaarvoice is a software company that powers the on-site reviews and ratings of some of the largest brands in the world, including Boots, Canadian Tire, Rubbermaid, and Samsung. When you see product reviews on the websites of companies like these, the reviews' functionality is often powered by Bazaarvoice. Matt Krebsbach, director of global public and analyst relations for Bazaarvoice, explains that reviews aren't just a way for consumers to express themselves. These sites also offer a tremendous amount of valuable information to potential customers. Reviews differ greatly from social media in this regard; he explains: "I may go onto Facebook and make a comment that I'm using my new MacBook Pro, but I'm probably not really sharing an awful lot of detail about it because I'm not really conditioned in that environment to engage with a brand, promote, or provide feedback. It's not the way in which most consumers leverage a network like Facebook. But if I'm providing a review, it's for the expressed intent of sharing my experience with that product, so it tends to be both very focused and very deep."

Having detailed information that educates consumers on your own website is wise, especially if your products or services are offered in multiple places online. In *Everyone's a Critic,* Bill Tancer writes: "Since more than 70 percent of consumers consult online reviews before making their purchase decisions, if you've chosen not to have reviews on your site, you're likely sending your customers to Amazon or another major online retailer to check reviews, and while they happen to be at your competitor's site, they may just decide to buy there."[14]

The District of Columbia encourages reviews and feedback from citizens through a system they built in partnership with the online feedback company NewBrand (now a division of Sprinklr), which aggregates and classifies the feedback that the city receives. More than half of the citizens' ratings and reviews come from a form on the city's website; the rest come from social media.[15] The NewBrand team reads each piece of feedback, and classifies it by administrative agency. Scores are then aggregated based on a good/bad/neutral system to form a real-time grade for each agency.

NewBrand president Kristen Kavalier explains that the city nudges citizens in multiple ways. "If you walk into a DMV [department of motor vehicles] today, you'll see a big poster and it encourages you to text your feedback, visit the website to provide feedback, or you can tweet them using a particular hashtag. It's fascinating to see how engaged the community is in wanting to provide feedback to the city, but also how wonderfully responsive the city has been."

The city uses these data internally with great fervor, and also publishes an external summary report card for citizens and the media. It's admirable for a government organization to be this open and transparent, especially with an owned review system. The concept of using your resources to collect feedback and then intentionally display potentially negative information in public is a tricky one to embrace. Companies want to hear from customers, but are also afraid of what customers might say.

As customer service consultant and author Steve Curtin says, "Feedback is the breakfast of champions. Nobody would publicly raise their hand in a boardroom and stand up and say, 'I resist feedback, especially when it's critical,' because that's not leadership, and that's not effectiveness. Nobody would support that. Yet as a practical matter, it happens all the time. Companies turn their back on feedback."

Perhaps those companies and those executives simply do not understand that psychologically, negative reviews can have a strong positive impact on consumers. More than two-thirds of customers trust reviews more when they see both good and bad reviews. Nearly all consumers (95 percent) suspect censorship or faked reviews when they don't see any bad scores, according to research from Reevoo, a Bazaarvoice competitor that handles online reviews for Kia motors in the UK, among other brands.[16] Beyond the persuasive effect on customers, also remember that your business *wants* negative reviews and feedback, because they tell you things you don't already know.

"Positive reviews tell a business what they are doing well, but they are probably already quite aware of what they believe they do well. So it's a validation. But negative reviews tend to really help inform a company of the areas where they can improve. Negative reviews really give companies that opportunity to make those significant, even if incremental, changes to their product or their service delivery that are very meaningful for consumers in the ongoing purchase process," says Krebsbach.

Hug Your Haters on Social Media

The opportunity to boost customer advocacy with a response may be greatest on forums, and the total number of consumer complaints may be highest on review sites. However, social media gets most of the attention among onstage customer service channels. The built-in immediacy of social media, and the ease with which consumers can complain and spread issues virally, make it the front line of any onstage program. I hope you'll answer every complaint, in every channel, every time. But if you have to pick and choose where to hug your haters anywhere beyond telephone and e-mail due to resources or other factors, it should probably be on social media.

Instead of watching customers naturally migrate from offstage to onstage channels, some companies embrace an alternate approach where social media customer service is encouraged as the very best way to interact with the company. Social media customer service software provider Conversocial propagates this philosophy with the #SocialFirst system they advocate to their corporate clients. As they write in their *Definitive Guide to Social Customer Service* (2015 edition), this approach includes five pillars:

> 1. *Proactive support for social customer service, making its existence widely known in marketing materials and sales/support collateral*
>
> 2. *Aggressive engagement aimed at exceeding customer demands*
>
> 3. *Interacting rather than reacting as a means to anticipate what customers want and need—before they tell you*
>
> 4. *Recognizing social media for its viral power and leveraging that reach to influence the market*
>
> 5. *Connecting with customers on a deeply personal and emotional level to build relationships and trust*[17]

These pillars can help any company embrace social media customer service, and also apply more broadly to any business looking to hug their haters.

Shutterstock is one of the world's largest sources for downloadable stock photos and images. Its website is an enormous resource for thousands of graphic designers and marketers, in companies of all sizes. Shutterstock uses many of the #SocialFirst principles in their social media customer service (also known as social care, especially in Europe), even when the haters come out in force.

In 2015 the Shutterstock website experienced an outage. Customers couldn't access anything. Immediately (because social media is the early warning detection system for most companies), Shutterstock started receiving tweets asking, "Is the site down?" Shutterstock then uploaded a "We're sorry" Web page to the site, but inadvertently used one that said, "The site is down for scheduled maintenance," which caused confusion and consternation among customers.

"People were not pleased," recalled content marketing manager Sarah Maloy. "So we got a lot of tweets, two or three per minute. Some of them more angry, some of them calling BS on us, saying, 'I don't believe this, Shutterstock.' So the way we handled those was we tried to be transparent, and we joked around."

Todd Kron is the online marketing manager for Xoom Energy in Charlotte, North Carolina. When the Shutterstock site was broken, he tweeted:

> @Shutterstock website is down. Down. Down. #ItsNot-MeItsYou

Within two minutes, Shutterstock responded with:

> @ToddKron #ItsNotYouItsDefinitelyUs . . . and we're working on it! Thanks for your patience today, Todd. [18]

This casual, sympathetic approach worked, and adhered to all five of the #SocialFirst principles. Shortly after the outage was fixed, customers started to send tweets praising the company for how they handled it, including one from Suzanne Deveney, a writer and designer in Chicago:

> *Need a great example of brand management? Check @Shutterstock responses about their outage: PERSONAL, timely & humorous #socialmedia #brand*[19]

"We got some really nice responses," Maloy said. "People really seem to appreciate that we're not just sending out the same robotic message over and over. That we're addressing each person individually. That we're shaping our messaging to fit whatever their particular scenario, as much as possible."

In addition to timely, personal responses, one of the techniques used by Shutterstock was to "pin" a response to the top of their Twitter and Facebook pages acknowledging the outage. This means that the first message encountered by visitors remained at the top of the tweet stream, even if other messages had been sent more recently. Pinning is a must-do in circumstances where you are receiving the same question or complaint over and over again in a short period of time (like an outage or other unexpected crisis scenario). I provide a more detailed examination of exactly how to handle crises in social media in the book I cowrote with Amber Naslund, *The NOW Revolution: 7 Shifts to Make Your Business Faster, Smarter, and More Social.*

Pinning responses can also help to remind customers that your social media support may not exist at all hours. When your social media customer service team logs off for the night, consider pinning a "We'll be back tomorrow at 9 a.m. If you need anything tonight, please e-mail . . ." or a similar message.

Carefully consider whether it makes sense for your social care team to ever be unavailable, though. Remember what happened with

British Airways when their hater bought ads slamming them for being offline, even though their hours of operation were clearly posted. Especially for larger companies, where customers may expect 24/7 social media service, having "off hours" may cause frustration.

Another common tactic among big companies is to create a dedicated account on Twitter solely for customer service. This separates customer care interactions from marketing messages. From a clarity perspective, this makes a lot of sense. But whose life is this making easier, the customer's or the company's? Discover does not have a separate customer service account on Twitter, and Dan Gingiss says that's intentional: "Discover is the only credit card company (in the U.S.)—and one of the few big companies out there at all—that has held on to this idea of a single Twitter handle. It is because it believes that customer service *is* the new marketing. And I don't believe as a customer that I should have to work to figure out what handle to use, either."

One of the reasons so many large companies are opting for a separate customer service presence on Twitter is that the attention paid to the service account is far less than the attention paid to the "main" account. Customer service accounts also tend to have fewer followers. By relegating customer service to a separate account, companies can also sweep accompanying negativity under the digital rug. I find this fascinating, and believe as Gingiss does that if you're good at service, you want everyone to see it. What do you have to hide?

Still, Twitter is enabling companies to do more service out of sight. The platform changed its policy on private, direct messages so that customers can send private messages to companies even if they don't follow those companies, and vice versa.[20] This creates an easy, hidden "back channel" for customer interactions that previously did not exist in a seamless way.

The Facebook equivalent of this back-channel approach is a special customer service module that companies can install as an application on their Facebook business page. This is what transportation marketplace uShip does, employing a Facebook version of its Get

Satisfaction customer support community to interact with customers directly on Facebook.[21]

There is no app or software required to use the Facebook private message system that enables correspondence between consumers and companies. Using Facebook for customer contact took another giant step when the technology was changed in 2015, allowing anyone to use the Facebook Messenger service, even those who don't have a Facebook account.[22] This is the next iteration in what I surmise is Facebook's long-standing strategic objective of becoming the de facto communication platform and replacement for e-mail.

The ability to operate both in public and in private makes social media customer service more powerful, and provides operational scaffolding for the #SocialFirst mantra. As we've seen, failure in off-stage customer service can create onstage haters. And now onstage social media channels give businesses the ability to handle customer complaints in private, similar to how offstage venues have always worked.

Certainly, if you must collect sensitive data from your customer to resolve her problem, relying on private messaging is a must. But because onstage haters want an audience, and social media gives them just that, the biggest opportunity for your business is to hug those haters out in the open. Show them who you are. Show them you care.

Wink Frozen Desserts embodies this philosophy with social media customer service that's so good, it blows customers' minds and wins their hearts.

Wink sells a vegan, dairy-free, gluten-free frozen dessert. An entire pint of Wink is just one hundred calories, which should perhaps serve as a clue that it isn't ice cream, even though Wink comes in flavors like vanilla bean, cinnamon bun, and iced latte. It's a polarizing dessert, as the following customer complaint posted to the Wink Facebook page illustrates. The message was posted by the Facebook account "Random Musings of a Barefoot Libertarian-Democrat Hippie," which might indicate that this consumer is looking for an audience not only when he complains but pretty much always. He wrote:

> *Just bought this hoping to be able to enjoy some ice cream while on a low-carb diet . . . too bad this "ice cream" (I put it in quotes because it tastes NOTHING like ice cream other than being cold) is absolutely disgusting! :(I got the "Cocoa Dough" version and literally licking the freezer burn "ice" shavings from the inside of the freezer would probably taste better than this! It's DEFINITELY going back to the store for a refund!*

I had a visceral negative reaction to this review for several reasons. First, the guy seems like a jerk. Second, he believes "nondairy dessert" equals ice cream, which places him in the "you get what you deserve" camp. Third, he wants to return something to a grocery store just because he didn't like the taste. Is that a thing that happens? Is that doable? I've consumed dozens of grocery items I didn't like over the years, but unless they were clearly defective in some way, I've never even considered asking for my money back. The natural inclination, of course, is to ignore this and assume no good will come of interacting with such a customer. But as our research found, that will make a bad situation worse, and it's not the Hug Your Haters way. Fortunately, Jordan Pierson is the chief marketing officer for Wink. He handles customer interaction in social media and beyond, and is reasonable and rational.

"When someone has something to say, they should be allowed to say it. It's tough whenever someone has something really negative to say about what we are doing. But regardless, our protocol is to try to publicly, visually respond to that in a nice and understanding way," he says.

Here's how he responded to the barefoot hippie:

> *Sorry to hear this Random Musings! While Wink is definitely not ice cream, we do aim for an ice cream like experience.*

> *The creator of Wink is a 25 year old named Gabe who has Celiac disease and dairy intolerance. We do recommend letting your pint sit out for a few minutes before you dig in. If the store you purchased Wink in gives you trouble with the refund please let us know! While we hope that everyone will love and enjoy Wink as much as we do, we realize that not everyone will. If we can help please send us an email to info@winkfrozendesserts.com. Thanks for giving Wink a try!*

Notice that he mentioned the inventor, Gabe—that's intentional. It humanizes the company and informs the consumer in one sentence. Very smart.

Pierson explains the approach: "I do try to educate them as much as I can, especially when someone compares it to ice cream. I'm always sharing Gabe's story because I find more often than not that nearly every person out there knows a Gabe, knows someone who can't have ice cream. And you don't think about it too often, especially if it's not someone who's going to go to an ice cream parlor with you or have ice cream at a party or something. For the most part, those people just quietly say no thank you. And I try to get people to understand that just because THEY didn't like it doesn't mean it's a bad product."

Jordan Pierson has the patience of Job and the disposition of your favorite primary school teacher. He is in the Hug Your Haters hall of fame. Are you ready to join him? Perhaps you're not entirely convinced. In the next chapter, I'll examine the five reasons you might not be adhering to these principles today.

You might be thinking, as we conclude this section, "What about other social media platforms? What about Instagram? Or Snapchat? Or Google Plus?" In the research for this book, we asked American complainers about their proclivity to complain via these channels. At this time, the portion of consumers using these other social outlets as a primary complaint mechanism is too slim to merit mention here. However, there are multiple *other* onstage complaint alternatives that are gaining in popularity with startling speed. I cover them in chapter 8.

(If you're enjoying *Hug Your Haters,* have a question, feedback, or just want to say hello, send me an e-mail right now at jay@jaybaer .com. I'll get back to you immediately.)

Chapter 5

Big Buts: 5 Obstacles to Providing Great Service

The Hug Your Haters approach is to answer every complaint, in every channel, every time. But that almost never happens. Very few businesses make that level of commitment to customer service, feedback acquisition, and hater embrace. Why? Why do we answer only some complaints, in some channels, some of the time? My interviews with more than forty companies for this book and my work consulting on customer experience and customer service initiatives finds five primary reasons why businesses are not hugging their haters today. Let's examine these objections and issues, see how many you recognize, and demonstrate how they are being overcome by businesses of all sizes. Whether you are a solopreneur, a 5-person business, a 1,000-person business, or a 100,000-person business, the same rules apply, anywhere in the world.

Obstacle #1: Too Many Channels

The Internet gives us many wonders, including real-time weather forecasts, live-streaming entertainment, and a cornucopia of cat antics on video. It also provides your customers many more venues to give you feedback. And they use these new options and alternatives every day, selecting one—and often several—based on convenience and circumstance. Research from Ovum finds that 74 percent of consumers use three or more channels when interacting with big companies for customer service issues.[1]

Google reviews. Yelp. Twitter. Facebook. Instagram. Industry-specific reviews sites and forums. Few of these were customer service factors even five years ago, and none of them existed twenty years ago. Plus there is a new breed of specialized messaging applications (discussed in depth in chapter 8). In combination, these relative upstarts have a major impact on how the public perceives you and on the success of your business.

If it feels like this proliferation of new channels and venues has caused customer service to spiral out of control, your instincts are correct. Businesses simply cannot dictate the terms of customer interaction and hope that consumers will fall in line. The balance of power in the relationship between company and consumer has forever shifted toward the customer.

Jennifer Larsen is the senior director of brand and reputation at MaritzCX, a customer experience software and research firm. She describes the shift like this: "It's not about forcing your customers to deal with you the way that you want to deal with them. It's about dealing with your customers in whatever way they choose to interact with you."

You may think you can continue to interact with customers only in offstage, legacy channels because your competitors aren't even doing that much. But in this era of information fluidity and instant mobile transactions, your competition isn't just the other companies that sell whatever you offer. Every company is your competition.

Once we experience a standard of excellence, we begin to expect that same standard, circumstances or company policies be damned.

Frequent travelers like me epitomize how customer experience impacts our expectations. The first few times I was upgraded to first class on a flight for accruing loyalty points, I was overjoyed. Given access to limitless snacks and beverages creates a *must eat and drink all the things* psychosis and a pervasive sense of satisfaction and privilege. That feeling fades, though. Now that I have loyalty points on par with the GDP of a small island nation, flying without an upgrade creates sadness and suspicion of the lucky souls who made the cut. "There's no way that guy has more miles than I do," I declare (in my head) as I slink back to the cheap seats.

Your customers are experiencing the same thing. Once they taste the snack-binging power of a twenty-four-hour Taco Bell, your decision to close at nine P.M. can be a real letdown. Once they get free shipping both ways from Zappos, it becomes increasingly difficult for your business to insist on charging for returns. If their complaint is answered on Twitter in five minutes by a big company like Discover, are they going to give your business a pass when you choose to ignore complaints in social media?

It doesn't matter what you and your direct competitors are doing, or prefer to do, in the realm of customer experience. The greatest businesses in the world are training your customers on what to expect, and they will eventually demand that you also meet that standard.

Embracing complaints and engaging with your customers everywhere isn't just an item on your to-do list; it's imperative for the future of your business. Remember that by 2020, customer experience will be more important than price.[2] The longer you wait to hug your haters across all channels, the harder the evolution will be, because as you delay, even more channels are emerging.

"The channel explosion will likely continue accelerating over the coming years with an ever-increasing number of concurrent channels expected to be made available in order to provide a world-class customer experience," says Bassam Salem, chief operating officer of MaritzCX.

Scott Wise from Scotty's Brewhouse has already made this shift, and is committed to soliciting and answering customer feedback in every possible venue. "We scrub the Internet for all messages and comments and complaints from everywhere. For us, it's Urbanspoon [a restaurant reviews site] and Yelp, and TripAdvisor. Also, Twitter, Instagram, Facebook, and Snapchat. You have to stay on top of everything that gets posted about you, anywhere it's posted," he says.

Wise is a visionary and an early adopter. He strives to be the first business in Indiana participating in each new channel as it emerges. As a result, he will never fall short of customers' expectations. He is an exception, of course, especially because he handles much of the customer interactions himself, dedicating ten-plus hours per week to it, personally. But even if you have another person, or many people, in your organization responding, the channel proliferation will impact you.

"The channel shift is coming," says Katy Keim from Lithium. "It just hasn't come yet as quickly as required to move funding and internal processes. The early visionaries see it, and are doing it. But there are a lot of other people who are like, 'Really? How important are these channels?' And those people are going to be caught really flat-footed, and eventually be at a competitive disadvantage."

Companies of all sizes often struggle to staff and support a new channel for customer interaction. Richard Binhammer was one of the pioneers of Dell's initial forays into social media customer care, and remembers the friction well: "Michael [Dell, the company founder] was very cognizant of the fact that customers had access to more and more platforms. We were being mentioned everywhere, and it needed to be addressed wherever the customer was. But the customer service department said, 'What do you mean? We already offer customers chat, e-mail, telephone, and online forums. We have enough channels.'"

Binhammer and Dell solved this dilemma by simply going around the legacy customer service infrastructure, at least at first.

"We pulled some of the best and brightest people in the company and set up a SWAT team that functioned outside of the customer service department. We associated the social media SWAT team with the communications team and formed a new group, called Communities and Communications, that was charged with helping customers in the support forums, but also finding discussions about Dell in blogs and social media and solving those problems," recalls Binhammer.

Eventually, as the social media program took root and became successful (dramatically reducing negative online mentions of Dell, according to Binhammer), the program was turned back over to the customer service department, where it was integrated and is still managed today.

Addressing new channels with a special, dedicated team is a fantastic way to prove the business value of broad hater hugging without putting the operational onus on an existing group that may be dubious and wary.

Your goal should be to follow Wise's lead and answer feedback everywhere. Eventually, you will do just that. But until then, be strategic and purposeful about which channels you use. Be very careful if you decide to experiment with a new channel. When you answer a few complaints here and there to "see how it goes," that experimental dabble can look like a commitment to a customer, and the expectation of future responses can be unwittingly set.

Large-scale complaints and feedback that indicate significant operations problems or a crisis should be answered everywhere, always. For routine customer feedback and day-to-day haters, if you do not have the internal commitments and resources necessary to do it right and do it well, don't do it at all. You are better off publicly stating that you "do not answer customer complaints on this channel" than participating in the venue in a scattershot, inconsistent fashion.

Obstacle #2: Too Much Feedback

There are definitely more haters than ever, especially online, where they are particularly active. From January 2014 to May 2015, there was an eightfold increase in customer complaints about business made on social media in the UK.[3] And between 2008 and 2018, the U.S. Department of Labor Statistics estimates that customer service representatives will experience the third-highest growth rate of any occupation.[4]

Mobile technology and the explosion of review sites and forums have made it easier than ever to provide feedback. Further, your participation in these venues actually creates more feedback, the way one barking dog spurs on every other dog within earshot to join the ruckus.

"When you start to engage with customers online, it causes more people to talk back. In general, when our customers implement a robust engagement strategy, they'll start to see a 30 to 40 percent increase in the total volume of commentary about their brand in the first few weeks or months," says Kristin Kavalier of NewBrand. "That's a really, really good thing because in general, when people talk online it's positive. So we want to encourage more chatter. And of course there are all kinds of related benefits like improvement in search engine results, particularly at the local level. And so online engagement is sort of the gift that keeps on giving. Once you've started interacting, there are all kinds of ripple impacts that we think are highly valuable."

Kavalier's point about most online feedback being positive is important. Nearly every company interviewed for this book, as well as research from Yelp and others, says the same. Laurie Meacham is the manager of customer commitment for JetBlue airlines and oversees the airline's customer service programs. She says that in social media, 60 percent of the customer comments are neutral—questions, mostly—30 percent are compliments, and just 10 percent are complaints. In an offstage channel like e-mail, the balance is different, with many more complaints than compliments. "We definitely get more compliments in social and more complaints in e-mail," Meacham observes.

Haters represent a small, critically important subset of all customer interactions online. And as discussed earlier in this book, much of what is considered an online complaint might never have been voiced in the pre-Internet era, because the magnitude of the issue wouldn't have matched the effort required to mention it. Julie Hopkins from Gartner describes the humdrum, narcissistic nature of many of our onstage "complaints": "I would imagine that the number of disappointed moments that are shared has probably gone way up because of the ease of putting your angst, frustration, and subpar feelings out into the social atmosphere," she says. "You can voice a foam latte art gone bad and say, 'Gosh I'm really disappointed because this was supposed to be a beautiful maple leaf and it just didn't turn out that way.' And yet that's not something that would have ever, ten years ago, been considered a complaint. And yet today, in the social space, the brand is going to sit there and someone is going to have to see it and deal with it."

Hopkins says we are training ourselves to be hypercritical about everything: "We have become a world of critics. We are able to evaluate and share our feelings in a moment's notice via different forms of media. We can tape it, we can shoot an image of it, we can shoot an image of it and retouch it. We can add a comment, and we can tag the brand in it. We can tag the brand and the actual location we're experiencing it. We are now trained and taught to put a critical eye toward everything."

Social media is a petri dish for First World problems.

Customers are now empowered to publicly log their latte problems, and company participation in onstage channels actually creates more chatter in more places. Consequently, the idea of "call deflection"—used by many large companies to justify the cost of robust social media customer service programs—is a myth. The notion is that customers will gravitate toward onstage channels over time, increasing the number of comparatively inexpensive interactions with companies online, while reducing the number of more expensive telephone and e-mail exchanges. Gartner reports that social media customer service personnel can deal with four to eight times the number of interactions than telephone advisers in the same time period.[5] In theory, it all makes sense. In reality, less so.

Customers' use of onstage channels has skyrocketed, of course, but the growth in the total number of interactions has essentially eliminated the presumed financial advantage of answering customers in less expensive, digital places. If you take ten phone calls that cost you six dollars each, it's an attractive proposition to shift five of those calls to Twitter interactions, at a cost of one dollar each. You'd save 41 percent! But what actually happens is that you now need to handle thirty Twitter interactions, and you end up with a channel shift, but no cost savings. This equation is exacerbated by the fact that the reduction in calls and e-mails doesn't always happen either.

Customer experience architect Esteban Kolsky explains this dynamic: "Every time we add a new channel to customer service, we always said, 'Oh it's about call deflection,' because it's the easiest way to prove value to customer service managers. That's all they want. They want to get rid of the calls, thinking that the calls are expensive. But every single time we found that, contrary to the claim of call deflection, we actually increased the number of calls. This is because people interact first with the company in social, but then are asked to call to actually resolve the issue."

Kolsky has it right, and the importance of this observation cannot be overstated. Your providers of online customer service must be able to actually address the problem and have the capacity to solve it whenever possible. If customers ask questions or log complaints on Twitter and you frequently require them to then call you to actually accomplish anything, you are doubling your workload. That scenario still has benefits, though. You are impacting customer advocacy, and the very public nature of your participation matters. You are also gleaning insights to make your business better and differentiating your business from that of competitors who don't respond publicly. Still, interacting with many of your customers multiple times across different channels is an expensive recipe for business improvement.

It takes resources to address the increasing tide of customer feedback. Hugging your haters isn't free. But some businesses embrace that wave and use it to make their companies better, or even use it as a marketing advantage. They want feedback from customers—the more the better—and they're willing to invest in collecting and addressing it.

As chronicled by John DiJulius in *The Customer Service Revolution*, Umpqua Bank in Portland, Oregon, works hard to harvest customers' opinions, even while they are visiting a branch location: "Every location has a phone in the lobby, with a sign next to it that reads LET'S TALK. Pick it up and you get connected to the office of CEO Ray Davis. You can pick up the phone and tell him what you think the bank is doing right and what you think it can do better, or you can ask him anything you'd like."[6] Umpqua is not a tiny, one-storefront bank either. As I write this chapter, the company has nearly four hundred locations.[7]

Le Pain Quotidien, the chain that turns hate into help by asking complainers to provide detailed reviews in exchange for gift cards, gets more feedback than ever, and loves it, according to Erin Pepper, director of marketing and guest relations: "One of my main goals when I got to the company was to increase our feedback, which we have. I've been here eleven months and we've doubled or tripled our feedback volume in the United States."

Alas, most companies aren't fully ready to embrace feedback and hug haters as much as Umpqua Bank and Le Pain Quotidien. Some businesses look at feedback volume not as an opportunity and an objective but as a signal that something is amiss. They want fewer complaints, not more. As Barlow and Moller wrote in *A Complaint Is a Gift:* "If a company's goal is to have fewer complaints this year than last, it is easier to accomplish than you might imagine. Staff will get the message and simply not report complaints to management. How many times have you delivered a written complaint to the front desk staff of a hotel and wondered if your complaint was passed on to the general manager?"[8]

Other businesses make tactical decisions to stretch their customer service resources further by using canned, robotic, or abrupt responses. It's faster to copy and paste than it is to craft a thoughtful, customized response. Is that time savings worth it? In some circumstances it may be, especially if you're giving the same information to different customers over and over, like in a service outage, for example. Note, however, that Shutterstock had a service outage and still responded to every customer with a customized, self-effacing reply.

Fundamentally, when you choose a rote-response system, you are doing so based on a value judgment. You decide it's not worth it to answer personally or in depth, and you don't. That was certainly the choice made by Pollon Flowers in Melbourne, Australia.

In 2015, Cheryl Lin Rodsted wrote this e-mail to her local florist:

> *Hello.*
>
> *I'm writing to request a refund on a bouquet of David Austen roses that my husband ordered and bought specially from your Melbourne store yesterday (April 14). The bouquet was wilted and the flowers were spotted and browning—I can bring them back and return them.*
>
> *It's also important that you know why this is so disappointing. A year ago I ordered my wedding bouquet from your store and as per email below, Nicholas promised me David Austen roses. My heart sank a little on the morning of our wedding day when I opened my bouquet box and found standard roses instead. Nicholas had promised me an "exquisite" bouquet and I was disappointed but naturally I chose to focus on having a happy day instead and it was such a great day that I was euphoric for weeks after! However later on*

our honeymoon the niggling picked up and I confided in my husband that the only thing I'd change from our wedding day was my bouquet and became a little obsessed with wanting to call up and ask why I was not provided the promised David Austen roses—naturally it's become a bit of a joke with us.

So my poor husband was trying to "make things right" by providing me with David Austen roses from your store. Not only did they not arrive on Saturday as initially promised in time for our anniversary, when we finally received them they were such a disappointing and sad-looking bunch that it's almost heart-breaking. I'd like to finally give you the chance to make this right by providing us with a full refund or perfect bunch of David Austen roses.

I look forward to hearing from you.

Cheryl

The e-mail reply from Pollon Flowers was succinct:

Don't ever contact us again.[9]

Cheryl Rodsted is certainly more passionate about rose specificity than most people, but she probably deserved better than a one-sentence dismissal. So as a thrice-spurned offstage hater, she took her grievances public and raised the stakes. She posted her e-mail and the florist's response to Facebook, Twitter, and Instagram, creating a torrent of "I'll never do business with them again" comments from nearby friends.

Instead of recognizing the error, Nicholas from Pollon Flowers compounded it, telephoning Rodsted, calling her a psychopath, and saying, "I know where you are, and I will come find you."[10] Yes, you should answer customer complaints, but, for the record, stalking customers and threatening them with bodily harm is not part of the Hug Your Haters success formula. Eventually, a different Pollon team member took over, and delivered new roses to Rodsted. This attempt to save time by sending a one-line response backfired, requiring sub- stantial effort to repair the relationship with not only the customer but also the growing crowd of online spectators.

Given that onstage channels can sometimes provide clues about the size of the customer's audience, some companies seek to be more efficient by replying to "influencers" instead of everybody. Using data like the Klout Score (a 1- to 100-point scale that purports to gauge social media participation and influence, owned by Lithium), companies can choose to respond only to comments from customers with a Klout Score above a certain threshold. This has some merit conceptually, as onstage haters with a built-in audience may be able to disproportionately help or hurt your business in comparison to the average customer. There are even offstage precedents for this type of segmentation, considering that loyalty programs (such as those in travel and hospitality) frequently offer special telephone support lines for members at a certain level.

But social media and review sites are public, and that makes it a dangerous game to pick and choose whom you answer, while also blurring the line between customer service and public relations. "Companies that only answer influencers are not providing customer service. They are engaging in reputation management," says Frank Eliason, who has held senior customer experience positions with Comcast and Citi.

Further, today's customers, especially the onstage haters, may easily notice the hopscotch nature of influencer-based answers, creating a potential for backlash.

"You don't want to pick and choose because people are smart. Communities are smart," James Degnan from Microsoft Xbox points out. "Let's say you and I both follow Xbox on Twitter, and Xbox has this model of picking and choosing. We both follow Xbox, we follow each other, and let's say I send a negative tweet to them, and you send a neutral 'engage with me' tweet, and they reply to you and don't reply to me. Your community will figure this out and think, 'Hey, you're going to address this guy because he's easier to address. You're not addressing me, and I can see that you're picking and choosing.' It creates more negative impact than companies realize."

Justyn Howard is the CEO of Sprout Social, a software tool used to find and interact with customers in social media. He explains the inadequacies of using influence as a filter for onstage interactions: "We run into a lot of organizations that say, 'Look, just show us the influential people so we can respond to those. Because we don't have time to respond to everybody.' That can't be the answer," he says. "You wouldn't only pick up your phone some of the time. If you have to add more people to be able to answer everyone, then do that. You can't just accept [complaint volume] as a problem you can't fix."

Instead of responding only to influencers, Jenny Sussin from Gartner recommends prioritizing customer interactions by issue type. She says, "I definitely think that there are posts that need to be prioritized. It could be the context of the discussion. It could be a topic that is quickly accelerating in terms of the overall number of mentions. It could be a topic that you've red-flagged as critical. So if you're Chobani yogurt and somebody is complaining about the smell of your product, that's a problem and you want to be alerted to that right away. If somebody says, 'I think there's a bomb on my train,' Metro-North might want to reply to that. But if somebody says, 'My train is running late,' they might say, 'Oh well.' It's all about context."

Another way to handle the rise in onstage complaints and customer feedback more efficiently is to ask your customers for help. We'll investigate emerging community-based support alternatives in chapter 8.

Obstacle #3: Offended by Feedback

A third reason businesses don't answer every customer is that the hate hurts too much. It's easy to take complaints personally and become bitter and cynical about the entire customer interaction process. This is especially true for small businesses.

Wade Lombard from Square Cow Movers recalls his first review—a one-star review on Yelp. "I read it and literally didn't sleep for three nights. How many people saw this review? It terrified me," he said. "And it made me want to stick my head in the sand and say, 'You know what? We can't fight this. We can't deal with online consumer reviews. We just need to keep working hard to make every client happy.' That fear is real. Don't say there's no reason for you to have that fear, because the fear is warranted. On the other hand, this isn't going away. Online consumer reviews are just growing, and to stick your head in the sand is the exact opposite of what you need to do. But I understand the fear, definitely."

The fear isn't triggered only by concern about the ramifications of a bad review; it's also biological, and wholly natural. In a *Harvard Business Review* article, Judith and Richard Glaser explain the neurochemistry of conversations, and why our first reaction to negativity is often to hide from it: "Chemistry plays a big role in this phenomenon. When we face criticism, rejection or fear, when we feel marginalized or minimized, our bodies produce higher levels of cortisol, a hormone that shuts down the thinking center of our brains and activates conflict aversion and protection behaviors. We become more reactive and sensitive. We often perceive even greater judgment and negativity than actually exists. And these effects can last for 26 hours or more, imprinting the interaction on our memories and magnifying the impact it has on our future behavior. Cortisol functions like a sustained-release tablet—the more we ruminate about our fear, the longer the impact."[11]

Remember that nearly four in ten onstage haters in social media who expect a response want it within an hour, yet the physiological impact of negativity on our brains and our judgment can last twenty-six hours.[12] This may explain, at least in part, cringe-inducing responses like Pollon Flowers' "Don't ever contact us again." It also underscores why your frontline customer service team needs to be filled with people who are equal parts level headed and even handed. That's often easier said than done, though, especially for small business owners who are forced to defend "their baby" against attacks that are easy to take personally.

In his book *The Customer Rules,* Lee Cockerell provides outstanding and practical advice for how to keep your wits about you in this situation:

> When a customer has a tantrum, it is vital not to take it personally. The anger is not about you—the customer doesn't even know you or care about you—it is about a situation. He's been disappointed or frustrated. Maybe she feels ripped off. The complaint may be totally unreasonable, and the reaction may be way over the top. Or not. Either way, it's not about you. It's about the circumstances. You're just the available outlet for the customer's rage. Fix whatever is wrong and you become the hero rather than the target. Keep this in mind, too: Everyone has problems that you don't know about. The customer screaming at you may have had the worst day of her life.[13]

Business owners sometimes choose not to respond to a complaint even when they don't feel personally attacked, but because they disagree with the customer's opinion and believe that replying adds credence where none is deserved.

"I think small business owners, and people in general, have pride, and there can be a belief that to respond to complaints is to dignify them. That to respond to complaints is to validate them. Some small businesses don't want to say they were wrong. They don't want to say they're sorry," explains Dave Kerpen from Likeable Media.

Unless it is fictitious or nefarious in some other way, however, every complaint is "true" from the perspective of the hater. Customers may have unrealistic expectations. There may have been extenuating circumstances. They may have been misled by their perspective or a simple misunderstanding, a scenario so common it often drives story lines of television shows like *Three's Company* and *Curb Your Enthusiasm* as well as the films of Akira Kurosawa and Alfred Hitchcock. In short, what the customer believes to have happened is what happened, in their head and in their world. Ignoring this and refusing to reply to complaints because you disagree with the assertions and do not want to unjustly dignify them is a textbook case of cutting off your nose to spite your face. Remember, haters aren't your problem. . . . Ignoring them is.

Every business has shortcomings on occasion. It's unfortunate that, of all days, that's when the onstage haters always seem to walk through the door. And sometimes you're simply victimized by your own success. Debbie Goldberg from Fresh Brothers Pizza lives that situation every day, as the lowest-rated among her fourteen locations may have a good reason for having slightly lower rankings.

"It's one of our highest volume stores. It's insanity there three nights out of seven. So in that kind of environment, stuff happens," she said. "So we look at ways to improve, and to get our timing down, and to maybe reduce the noise in the dining room, or get the food out faster to our dine-in customers, that kind of thing. But at a certain point, at that speed, there are mistakes that are going to happen. So we look at our reviews really carefully and analyze, for example, if a customer mentions a specific employee by name in a negative way or even a positive way. Is there a customer service problem? Are we having a cooking issue? Are people talking about the pizzas in this specific way? In the case of this store, I think it's a great store because we overall hear great feedback from people. But because it has such a high volume, it also gets a lot more reviews," she explains.

Whether online or offline, responding to customer complaints—even if you don't believe them to be accurate—is the best approach.

Subaru of Wichita, a new and used vehicle dealership in Kansas, created a wave of attention based on how they hugged their offstage haters.

It all started with some drywall. In 2014, the dealership spent $1.5 million to refurbish their facility. Seeking to keep all project revenue in the local economy, the company employed a local contractor, used a local bank for funds, and sourced local suppliers. After the project was completed, the trouble began.

Protestors on behalf of Carpenters' Union Local 201 appeared, setting up an enormous sign on the public easement in front of the dealership. The sign, approximately thirty feet long, read SHAME ON SUBARU OF WICHITA, with smaller notations of "Labor Dispute" in the top corners.

Evidently, a small portion of the remodeling project required new drywall. The local contractor and construction firm solicited several bids for the work from Wichita-area drywall professionals, and selected the lowest bid, which came from a nonunion business, triggering the protests. In addition to the sign, the union also posted a flyer on its website, taking the dealership to task.

Subaru of Wichita didn't agree that they were "desecrating the American way of life" (the union's words), given that they had made every effort to use local suppliers. With that in mind, the business didn't take it personally, but they did respond, first online by addressing each of the union's claims on the dealership website, and then offline.[14]

Says media and marketing manager Aaron Wirtz, "Online or offline, we always want to respond in ways that are in keeping with who we are as a company. One of the tenets of our company is that we are a golden rule dealership. We do unto others as we would want them to do unto us. But it's also a big part of who we are, to not just simply take whatever is thrown at us. On the union banner, we acknowledge your right to say those things. However, since we disagree, we are going to respond in ways that are in keeping with who we are. So it's not about attacking with nastiness or hostility. It's about responding in ways that are in keeping with us."

Wirtz and his team created their own banner. Mimicking the union banner's font, size, and color scheme and placed right next to the union's version, it read FOR HAVING UNBEATABLE PRICES, with notations of "indisputable" in the top corners. Every day for six months, Wirtz set up the banner each morning, and packed it up at the end of the day. Like a postman with ironic sensibilities, Aaron Wirtz displayed his response banner through rain, sleet, snow, and sunshine.

He hugged his haters, and it worked. In this instance, haters were not customers per se, but vendors. But the same dynamics apply.

In the aftermath, Wirtz says awareness of the dealership increased dramatically. Online reviews from customers specifically mentioned that the dealership would not have been on their shopping list had it not been for the union response sign.

Aaron Wirtz understands that complaints are an opportunity to set the record straight, to differentiate, to build pride, to keep your customers, and to gain new ones. There's no need to try to quash negativity. This is especially true in review sites, where a handful of negative reviews can actually benefit your business. It's a paradox, but it's true. A study from UK software firm Reevoo found that consumers spend four times as long on websites when they read bad reviews, and purchase 67 percent more than the population as a whole.[15]

Andrew DiFeo, the owner of a Hyundai automobile dealership in St. Augustine, Florida, understands this perception factor. Daniel

Lemin shared DiFeo's story in his book *Manipurated*. Once DiFeo realized how important the review site DealerRater was to his potential customers, he focused his marketing budget, time, and effort on this and other review sites. "We need bad reviews," said DiFeo. "It's an odd thing, but it adds credibility."

By addressing customer service issues and responding to negative reviews, he turned around his company's fortunes. In fact, Dealer-Rater named his business Dealer of the Year for three years in a row, from 2010 to 2012. Most important, his dealership more than doubled its sales volume.[16]

When the existence of relevant negativity increases the perceived veracity of reviews overall, why would you go out of your way to make sure you don't get any negative reviews? Why would you try to pull a stunt like the owners of the Union Street Guest House did?

In 2014, the boutique hotel and events center in Hudson, New York, posted a policy on its website that claimed:

> *If you have booked the Inn for a wedding or other type of event anywhere in the region and given us a deposit of any kind for guests to stay at USGH there will be a $500 fine that will be deducted from your deposit for every negative review of USGH placed on any Internet site by anyone in your party and/or attending your wedding or event.*

Whoa! A five-hundred-dollar fine for every negative review? That redefines cheeky customer service policies. Perhaps predictably, this didn't end well. The *New York Post* noticed the Web page and ran a story about it in the newspaper and online, creating a firestorm of more than three thousand one-star reviews for USGH on Yelp.[17,18] The fraud team at Yelp removed nearly all the reviews, since it could not be determined how many came from actual guests. However, nearly a year before the *Post* story, Yelp members were complaining that they had actually been contacted by the hotel seeking a five-hundred-dollar payment for a negative review.[19] Though hotel owner

Chris Wagoner claimed it was "a joke," not only was the damage done but perhaps it was symptomatic of a larger problem with the hotel. As of this writing, the hotel has fifty-four total Yelp reviews, forty-five of them with only one star, and a cancellation policy that reads like a nuclear disarmament treaty.

Obstacle #4: Fear of Getting Scammed

Because they have the virtual audience they seek, onstage haters' behavior can feel like an extortion scheme. "Do this for me . . . or else" is the general thrust of some of these interactions, with haters believing they can hold businesses hostage simply because social media, review sites, and forums include onlookers. This is especially prevalent among "influencers" who believe that citizenship and the laws of society should be amended due to their ability to craft 140-character witticisms on Twitter.

This doesn't happen often, but it does happen. And when it happens, companies often say, "Good riddance, that was a bad customer." This makes inadequate customer experience and refusal to answer complaints institutionally permissible, as long as it was "the customer's fault." Lee Cockerell recounted seeing this "bad customer" fallacy play out during his time at the Walt Disney theme parks in his book *The Customer Rules:* "From time to time over the years, a customer would complain to me that a frontline employee had been belligerent. When I asked the employee what happened, I'd usually be told that the customer was wrong about the facts, or had been abusive, or was trying to cheat the company. Most of the time, the employee believed it was better to lose a bad customer than appease one. They were surprised when I told them there's no such thing as a 'bad' customer."[20]

As we discovered in the introduction to *Hug Your Haters,* Debbie Goldberg at Fresh Brothers answers almost every complaint, in every channel, and routinely delivers gift cards to unhappy customers. She's heard, over and over, that one of the reasons businesses don't get involved with customers (especially in social media and review sites) is because customers will try to extort the company for free goods and services. She is unmoved by this argument.

"It makes me laugh. These people are providing feedback to your business for free, so rewarding them with a ten- or fifteen-dollar gift certificate makes them feel great, first of all. But it's just really smart. It's like having these brand ambassadors out there, and you want to keep them going. You want to keep them giving you thumbs-ups and shout-outs, and it's really an easy way to build a relationship with people, and to get them to be even further invested, emotionally, in your company," she says. She also acknowledged that there are customers looking to take advantage of her largesse: "We do see times where we think a person is fishing for a gift card, but you've got to go with the benefit of the doubt. We have a tracking system where we know who we're sending gift certificates out to. If we see somebody that's a repeat, we'll look and see why and investigate. But overall, it's definitely not my first concern."

It's not Gary Vaynerchuk's first concern either. His company, VaynerMedia, manages the online interactions for dozens of very large multinational brands. In an interview with me, when asked about the dangers of customers trying to get a discount, he said, "Who cares? That's the cost of doing business. I wish everybody would give away free gift cards because it would provide a better cost of new customer acquisition than marketing does. It's literally better to give away free gift cards to everybody than to do a broad, expensive marketing campaign."

Is the distribution of a few undeserved gift cards (or whatever the equivalent might be in your business) sufficient grounds to not hug your haters? Not every customer has pure intentions, but is that a legitimate rationale to ignore them? Many experts and business owners say it is not.

And on the flip side, if it makes you feel ethically compromised to provide a freebie to someone who may not warrant it, simply don't. If a customer threatens to slam you on Twitter, or write a negative review, or turn their friends into a pitchfork-wielding, angry mob on Facebook, maybe you just shouldn't give in to him. Let him go onstage. Because if you're committed to answering every complaint, in every channel, every time, you'll have the chance to tell your side of the story. And the audience almost always respects the truth.

As Wade Lombard from Square Cow Movers tells it, "One out of maybe five hundred clients truly are malicious and deceitful. They want to take advantage, and they aren't reasonable. But, man, 99 percent of them are just wonderful people. And so I'm going to take those odds to Vegas every time."

Obstacle #5: No Customer Experience Culture

Let's face it: choosing whether to hug your haters isn't as much about knowing how to do so as it is about whether doing so aligns with the values of your business. Every company says that customer satisfaction is its most important objective, yet its actions demonstrate otherwise. It's a paradox, but I find that companies that feel the need to make public statements about customer experience being important are usually the companies for which that clearly is not the case. It's like what my former colleague the advertising executive Roger Hurni told me about Applebee's restaurants: "If you have to use your tagline to tell people you're the neighborhood bar and grill, you're definitely not the neighborhood bar and grill."

Joe Gagnon is senior vice president at Aspect, a company that helps large corporations improve customer service with software and optimization services. He says some companies simply do not prioritize satisfied customers, and have no qualms about it. "In the few cases when the cost of customer acquisition is lower than the cost of retention, there is almost a disincentive to customer satisfaction." Gagnon relayed a quote from a fast-food franchise operator who told him, "I don't really care about customer satisfaction. I just want to serve them food and have them pay me."

As a consumer, when you encounter the opposite, a business that really and truly puts customers first, they don't even have to tell you it's so, because you can feel it. These are the company cultures where delivering a great customer experience is baked in at the molecular level. In an instant, you can probably name five local or national companies that always make you feel like a valued customer. It's not a coincidence that those companies are also often great at customer service, and committed to hugging their haters.

We can easily name customer experience cultures because they are rare. Their scarcity contributes mightily to their memorability. These companies are exceptional, in the truest definition of the word: they are exceptions.

And the financial impact of a focus on customers is massive. A 5 percent increase in customer retention can boost profits by 25 to 85 percent. That's not a new discovery; it was published in a *Harvard Business Review* case study in 1990.[21] So we've known that a focus on customer experience makes sound business sense for twenty-five years or more, but the companies that execute on it are still outliers. Why?

"You know how they say 'The fish rots from the head?' Your customer journey is driven from the top down. This is absolutely a cultural thing. There is not a problem in the world that can't be solved technologically, but the best technology is going to do nothing for you unless you have a culture of customer excellence," says Michael Maoz of the research and advisory firm Gartner.

JetBlue airlines has such a culture, as evidenced by a story told by social media customer service manager Laurie Meacham about a passenger who had been tweeting before her flight. According to Meacham, the passenger was not tweeting at JetBlue directly but just tweeting in general. It was obvious from her previous tweets that she had been having a rough time in life. Her last tweet before boarding was "I'm so looking forward to getting the Popchips." Jet-Blue usually serves free snacks on flights, and Popchips are a customer favorite. Unfortunately, the plane was out of Popchips and the passenger tweeted her disappointment, using the in-air Wi-Fi connection.

This is a classic example of indirect haters, those hidden complainers that most companies never find, much less act upon. "She wasn't really talking to us or complaining to us," says Meacham. "This was just her narrative. So we packaged up a box of Popchips with a little note and we mailed it to her home. She sent a tweet a few days later with a photo, saying, 'Look at what JetBlue sent me!' It was our way of sort of making up for it. And, you know, sometimes it's better to take things offline."

Meacham emphasizes that none of these beyond-the-norm interactions requires permission from multiple people at JetBlue, where working "off script" is valued far more than adhering to the script. "It's exactly these sorts of spontaneous things that we want to empower our team members to recognize. They just find them, and act on them," she says.

Martin Shervington from Plus Your Business calls this the culture of "sincere hospitality" and notes that there are particular attributes of companies that have this culture. Everyone in the organization feels like they are in customer service, even if they aren't specifically assigned those duties. All team members are empowered to solve a customer's problem at any time, the way they are at the Ritz-Carlton hotel chain and other customer-focused brands. Even executives or owners interact with customers.

You might think it's easier for small business owners to connect with customers than it is for large company executives, and you're right. But it's by no means impossible for executives to talk to customers in a big organization; they just have to want to do it badly enough. Pella Windows and Doors wants to do it, and does.

"Our founder, Pete Kuyper, who got this company going ninety years ago, always thought that the best thing you can do is to take care of the customers, and there are numerous stories about him bending over backward to take care of things. That's always been part of our DNA," says Pella's vice president of marketing, Elaine Sagers. "Monthly, our executives call a random selection of unhappy customers to talk about their experiences with us. Sometimes it can be really painful because it's often simple stuff that goes wrong," she says. "We now start every one of our monthly business meetings [a meeting with the most senior leaders in the company] with a good customer letter and a bad customer letter. We've also played recordings from the call center so you can hear the emotion in our customers' voices around what's been happening with their jobs and their homes."

The large tax preparation company Jackson Hewitt has also embraced customer experience and involved its senior executives as well. "Dave Prokupek came on board as CEO in 2014 and he has a fierce passion for the customer, and for the customer being happy and being heard," says Vada Hill, Jackson Hewitt's chief marketing officer. "I'm a big believer in that's an important part of my job that I reach out to customers. I call customers on the phone. In executive discussions I've printed out the Facebook accounts of certain customers who were not being served well, with an eye toward putting a face to an unhappy customer. I think that it's really important that as an executive team we are sensitized to the people behind the complaints. These are real people, these are people on whom our livelihood as a business depends, and it's very important that we meet their needs and that they feel that they've been heard," Hill explains.

If you're going to embrace customer experience and hug your haters, it certainly helps to have an executive team that believes in sincere hospitality, as do Hill, Sagers, and their respective CEOs. It also helps if the company puts its money where its mouth is, and most simply do not.

In nearly all companies (but perhaps not in businesses focused first on customer experience), resources are disproportionately expended on getting customers, not keeping them.

Globally, $500 billion each year is invested in marketing, compared with just $9 billion in customer service.[22] Katy Keim from Lithium describes the gap this way: "Marketing has the funding, but not the capabilities. Customer service has the capabilities, but not the funding."

Global Expenditures for Marketing and Customer Service

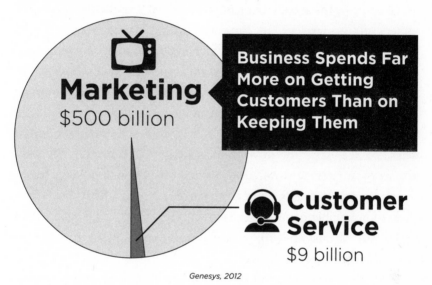

Marketing
$500 billion

Business Spends Far More on Getting Customers Than on Keeping Them

Customer Service
$9 billion

Genesys, 2012

One of the ways to close that gap is to constantly prove the value of service and complaint resolution, a measurement imperative that has bedeviled the customer experience industry for years.

Carine Clark, president and CEO of MaritzCX, says the metrics problem is finally being fixed. "Customer experience programs in the past were missing a critical element—a measurable impact on business outcomes. It was almost as if these programs were a ship without a rudder, aimlessly delivering scores, data, and statistics to bewildered employees and busy executives," she says. "But today's programs are different. Their direction is set by strong, visionary strategies that focus on outcomes. Today's programs directly impact the most relevant boardroom measurements: customer retention, revenue growth, profitability, and employee loyalty. Business leaders and employees inherently understand that improving the customer experience makes sense. On a logical level, it really is the baseline for every business: making customers happy. Often business leaders get distracted, thinking that their business is something else, like design, pricing, presentation, or quality. These are all previews to the real show, customer retention based on the overall customer experience."

Clark is right. A commitment to customer experience keeps customers and grows revenue. But measuring that relationship can be time consuming and expensive, which is why so many customer service and customer experience programs use other data points as surrogates for financial gain. These include metrics like Net Promoter Score, which charts the likelihood of customers to recommend the business to a friend or colleague. Net Promoter Score methodology was also the basis for how we measured the customer advocacy impact of answering complaints among offstage and onstage haters when we conducted the research for this book. Other businesses chart total number of customer interactions per channel, which is how KLM and Microsoft Xbox know precisely how many tweets they answer each week.

For many years, customer service organizations that were primarily focused on telephone interactions charted their "handle time," the time needed to answer the phone and bring the issue to a close. This feels like an anachronism in today's world, where customers expect a quick response across many channels. Discover, Jackson Hewitt, and KLM pay close attention to this "response time" and use it as a key success measure, rather than handle time.

Customer experience architect Esteban Kolsky doesn't believe either measure is sufficient, and that we should be tracking "resolution time" because it represents what the consumer really wants and needs. "It's about answers. People want answers and an answer equals value. The faster, better, and more complete, more accurate answer that you deliver, the more value you deliver. That's what it comes down to. So figure out what's the best way to deliver the best answer, via the best way possible at the right time. That's value to the customer," he says.

Joe Gagnon believes the best measure is "customer effort." "What customer service is really about, and what we try to do at Aspect, is connect questions to answers," he says. "And we should be measuring how easy (or difficult) it is for the customer to get that answer," he says. "If it's easy enough, you'll start to see it emerge in customer comments like 'I can't believe how easy that was.'"

Surveys are one of the other systems used by both small and large businesses to gauge the effectiveness of their customer service. You no doubt have received requests to provide feedback through a survey, often "invited" (like it's a party with an open bar) to participate via an e-mail blasted to you after your most recent transaction with a business.

I make it a habit to answer these requests to complete surveys. Whether I'm asked to rate my recent chicken wing experience or grade my local car dealership, I'm happy to oblige because I find these surveys fascinating. I also find them to be almost universally terrible.

Not long ago, I had a poor experience at a Las Vegas casino hotel. I don't want to tell you which one, but it has an enormous lion at the front entrance. I received a standard e-mail blast with a link to the post-stay survey. Eager to share my thoughts, I clicked to open the survey and discovered a customer satisfaction crime scene. The survey was more than sixty pages long and took more than forty minutes to complete. Only at the very end did the hotel ask for my actual feedback, and even then it was in a truncated and perfunctory fashion. What did the other fifty-plus survey pages contain? Question after question after question about marketing and Las Vegas strip competitors. "What restaurants did you visit on our property?" they asked, followed by an enormous list. "What restaurants did you visit elsewhere in Las Vegas?" they asked next, followed by a list that dwarfed the first one.

This is not customer service measurement. This is not embracing customer feedback. It's marketing and market research. There are many times and places where those questions and conversations are appropriate. The first 75 percent of a guest satisfaction survey is not one of those times.

Beyond their wholly soulless nature that lacks a shred of humanity or nuance, the issue with some surveys is where the results go and how they are used. It's entirely possible that one or more surveys are being sent to your customers at this very moment. Who has access to the results? How is that information used? Are trends charted? Are summaries provided on a regular basis to the customer service and operations teams? Are key findings presented to executives for discussion, as is the case at Pella and Jackson Hewitt?

If you're going to make use of surveys, make use of the data they capture. Otherwise, you're just setting up a false expectation among your customers that you are listening, when in reality you're deflecting.

We've seen that a customer experience culture with a commitment to sincere hospitality requires leadership from owners and/or senior executives. It also requires resources, as hugging your haters isn't an inexpensive proposition. You need relevant measurement and metrics as well.

The last thing you need is permission to say you're sorry. And that's not a given, especially in big companies.

Frank Eliason has seen it firsthand. "One of the first unofficial rules often taught to customer service professionals in large companies is the inability to say 'I'm sorry.' Management instructs that saying 'I am sorry' is somehow admitting fault. Always remember that how you communicate to your employees sends a message. Sometimes that message may be about risk, other times it could be about profits and the way that the message is received will impact how you treat your customers, even if it was never intended to be that way."[23]

In some corners of the business universe, anyone interacting with customers is prohibited from saying (or typing) an apology, because it is believed—by particularly Draconian attorneys—that it could weaken the company's position in a legal proceeding. I am not a lawyer, but that feels wrong to me. Dave Kerpen (also not a lawyer) feels the same way. "Attorneys might not love the words 'I'm sorry,' but the reality is 'I'm sorry' is not an admission of liability, it's a declaration of empathy," he says.

I like the concept of "declaration of empathy," but is there legal justification to the idea of never saying "I'm sorry"?

"In the words of Charles Dickens, 'If that's the law, then the law is a ass,'" says Michael Lasky, an attorney and litigator with the Davis & Gilbert law firm in New York City. Lasky specializes in public relations, advertising, and e-commerce law. "Any notion that 'I'm sorry' is an admission of liability is far too simplistic and is definitely an overreaction. Should companies be careful about what they say, especially in a public forum? Sure. But I don't think the answer is simply you can never respond to negative complaints, and you can never say 'I'm sorry.'"

Some businesses won't allow their representatives to say "I'm sorry," but they certainly will allow their representatives to tell the customer no. If you start to pay attention to how often you say no, whether due to "policy" or for some other reason, the results can be staggering.

Ameriprise Financial, for example, asks its customer service representatives to capture every instance in which they are forced to tell a customer no. While auditing the no's, the company found many legacy policies that had been outmoded by regulatory changes or process improvements. During its first year of "capturing the no's," Ameriprise modified or eliminated twenty-six policies. It has since expanded the program by asking frontline customer service agents to come up with other process efficiencies, generating $1.2 million in savings as a result.[24]

Maybe it's the proliferation of feedback mechanisms. Or the volume of feedback is too high. Or you take haters' complaints personally and ignore them. Maybe you're afraid of getting scammed or extorted by the rogue customer. Perhaps you don't have the leadership and the culture to support answering every question, in every channel, every time. It's probably some combination of these obstacles that is preventing you from truly hugging your haters. But each can be overcome, and each is being overcome by companies, large and small.

But once you've decided to embrace complaints, how do you actually do it, day to day? What matters and makes a difference? Let's find out, starting with how to handle offstage haters.

Chapter 6

H-O-U-R-S: The Playbook for Hugging Offstage Haters

As we saw in the Hatrix in chapter 3, offstage haters almost always expect a response. After all, they are seeking an answer. Giving them what they need not only increases customer advocacy but also prevents them from raising the stakes, taking it public, and morphing into onstage haters.

You know how to answer a telephone and reply to an e-mail. But let's go beyond the basics and examine the five ingredients of truly excellent offstage interactions.

To help you remember these five ingredients, I've created a handy pneumonic: H-O-U-R-S.

Be **H**uman
Use **O**ne Channel
Unify Your Data
and **R**esolve the Issue
with **S**peed

Be Human

It is easy to fall into the trap of thinking of your customers as a collection of data points, especially when so many of the typical offstage measurement approaches look at average handle time or total e-mail inquiries. It's not unusual, especially in large companies, to gloss over the fact that every "5 percent increase" or similar trend is comprised of dozens or hundreds or thousands of individual customers with unique lives and circumstances. Nobody is calling or e-mailing your business for its raw entertainment value. They have problems and they need help. And the very best way to begin hugging those haters is to show your humanity while respecting their humanity.

Making that human connection work every time, and avoiding the displacement of the personal in favor of the procedural, very much requires a strong culture and continuous reinforcement.

According to Steve Curtin, author of *Delight Your Customers,* Delta airlines has an interesting and effective method for ensuring that their frontline responders interact with humanity. The company emphasizes "being present" when serving customers, and says that if Delta representatives cannot remember their last three customers, they are just processing, not being human. "Employees who just process or simply go through the motions may be the single greatest barrier to companies achieving consistently high levels of customer satisfaction," Curtin wrote in a blog post about the Delta initiative.

He also says that each team member has not just one job, but two: "Every employee's job is made up of both job *functions* (the duties associated with a job role) and job essence. Issuing a boarding pass is a job function. Making a personal connection is job essence. Many employees focus almost exclusively on job function. The result is accurate work that conforms to standards. In the process, however, customers often receive homogeneous, bland and uneventful service during the transaction and no personal connection is made."[1]

To increase efficiency, scripted telephone and e-mail responses were the norm for many years in big companies, but that trend is reversing as organizations come to better understand the benefits of being human and working "off script."

Dave Fish, PhD, senior vice president for expert services at MaritzCX, explains this development: "Standard programs were very popular for a while; greet people in X amount of time, answer the phone in Y rings. However, it was a very mechanistic approach that dehumanized people, treating them as machines versus what people really want to interact with, a human being! The first step in consistency is to have a very clear brand. What do you stand for? What is important to your organization? Does everyone know that? Do they believe it and live it? The next step is recruit, select, and promote to that brand. Getting the right people is absolutely critical in building a world-class organization that reinforces your brand. Next, rather than giving employees specific operating standards, give them guidelines and empower them to use their judgment. That will make for happy employees and happy customers. It will also increase retention of your staff, which we know is directly related to increased customer loyalty."

While you certainly should seek to be human in your interactions with customers who call or e-mail to complain, the power of humanity can also be deployed in proactive scenarios, to prevent complaints from occurring at all. Dr. Glen Gorab, a New Jersey–based oral surgeon, is the master of this dual approach.

Dr. Gorab differentiates his practice by interacting with his patients when there are complications, and in more than thirty years as a surgeon, he has never been sued. But what's even more interesting is what he's been doing for nearly twenty of those years: using humanity to build bonds with patients before they ever walk through the door.

Every weekend, Dr. Gorab personally telephones every patient who is coming to his office for the very first time in the coming week. It's usually four to twelve calls, placed without fail every Saturday or Sunday. The impact of this simple gesture is extraordinary.

"I want to let them know that I'm a real person. I'm not a doctor, I'm on their level. I actually care about their care. So taking the time on a Saturday or a Sunday where I'm really not doing much or just driving in the car? It really blows people away," Dr. Gorab explains. "They can't believe it. They say, 'No doctor has ever done this for me before. That's really nice.'"

He realizes that the entire process of visiting his office is fraught with doubt, and he seeks to alleviate those concerns in advance, rather than in arrears.

"The experience of going to an oral surgeon is not like going to get a mani-pedi. It's not a pleasurable experience. People usually are dreading it. So inherently, there is always a lot of apprehension in going to a visit like this. That apprehension can manifest itself in fear, anger, and confusion. So I call and say something like, 'Hi, this is Dr. Gorab (although I always introduce myself as Glen when in the office). I understand we have an appointment Tuesday afternoon at two P.M.? I like to call my patients ahead of time just to introduce myself and ask if you have any questions prior to your appointment.' They say, 'Oh, that's very nice. I never expected a doctor to call.' By the time they come to the office, they're already your friends and they're on your side. So it's really all about communication and letting people know that you really care about them."

Dr. Gorab says he consistently sees new patients who specifically reference the weekend calls he makes as a reason for selecting him as their oral surgeon. "They call and say, 'Yeah, my friend Shirley told me that you called her the weekend before her appointment.'" The human touch has clearly led to increased customer advocacy for Dr. Gorab.

Use One Channel

Offstage haters select a particular channel because they believe it's the best and most convenient way to get a problem solved. It's a strategic choice and customers mentally evaluate their options and choose to call or to e-mail. So when they interact with a business in their pre- |131| ferred channel and are told that they have to use a wholly different channel to actually get the answer they seek, frustration bubbles over like a diet soda poured on a turbulent flight. If customers contact you in a venue of their choosing, you should do your very best to answer their questions and provide assistance in that same venue.

Research chronicled in the *Harvard Business Review* shows that 57 percent of customers contacting businesses report having to switch from the Web to the phone, and 62 percent report having to repeatedly contact the company to resolve the issue.[2]

Customers hate offstage channel switching. More than one-quarter of all customers say the most important element of good service is getting their issue resolved in a single transaction. That's more important than accuracy and politeness.

The satisfaction that accompanies having their problem solved on the first try isn't just a psychic benefit either. It equals real financial gain for the companies that can offer one-channel resolution.

Customers who receive a first-contact resolution are nearly *twice* as likely to buy again from a brand, and four times more likely to spread positive word of mouth about it.[3]

Answering complaints and solving problems in a single channel gets more difficult when haters quickly jump between onstage and offstage channels without waiting for a resolution from either. This "shotgun" approach often creates confusion inside the company, and can actually slow response times while the different complaints are synched and ownership of the issue is settled.

When a situation does require a customer to switch channels, it's important for the representative handling the second (or third) inquiry to not accidentally indict their brethren who were unable to solve the problem the first time. Janelle Barlow and Claus Moller describe this cautionary tale in *A Complaint Is a Gift* like this: "Service providers need to carefully explain what happened without sounding as if they are attempting to pass blame onto someone else. They can probably accomplish this by saying, 'I'm going to take responsibility for this, even though several people were involved. We need to find out what happened so I can solve this problem for you.'"[4]

South Africa's Nedbank solved this issue by issuing an "Ask Once" promise, which guarantees that the representative who picks up the phone will own the customer's issue from start to finish. According to CEO Tom Boardman, "The overarching Ask Once promise ensures that the customer will only ask once, and the Nedbank person handling his or her query will promptly get it resolved."

After rolling out the Ask Once promise, Nedbank was named the continent's best bank for customer service two years running in the Ask Afrika Orange Index.[5]

Unify Your Data

A related challenge for businesses—and an extreme annoyance for consumers and complainers—is the inability to provide customer service representatives easy access to all information necessary to resolve problems.

How maddening is it when you call a company and enter your account number on your phone's keypad, only to have to immediately repeat your number once you're connected with a representative?

Why did they ask for the number the first time? Is this a joke? An intelligence test? I hate this. You hate this. Research proves it: 85 percent of consumers feel negative toward businesses that require them to provide information multiple times.[6] That statistic causes me to think these two things: "Of course" and "Who are the 15 percent who are not bothered by this, and how do they have so much free time?"

For some customers this isn't just a minor annoyance either. More than a quarter say it would be enough to make them consider leaving for a competitor.[7]

Says Bassam Salem, chief operating officer of MaritzCX, "In addition to dictating the communication channel by which they will reach you, customers want and expect you to be able to integrate all channels—that means honoring the same offers on the Web as in the store and moving between channels without hassle. As a consumer, I know I would like information given over the phone to be on file when I shop in the store or place an order via the provider's website— but all too often I am disappointed."

That's certainly a more common shortfall among big companies, but smaller businesses face similar challenges. Debbie Goldberg from Fresh Brothers Pizza says they keep a list of gift cards they've sent out to haters and fans on Yelp and beyond. But do store managers have access to that same list? How much contact do the people answering the phone and e-mails have with the personnel interacting with customers in the real world?

Data fragmentation is a by-product of two realities. First, different people or groups or departments are assigned to handle customers in distinct channels. Second, much of the software used to manage legacy, offstage channels wasn't designed to also provide real-time visibility into online, onstage customer interactions.

The first issue can be addressed by having a single dedicated group address all customers in all channels. But in most cases, the trend is swinging the other way, with the formation of dedicated teams to handle only social media, with separate teams handling telephone, e-mail, or a combination of the two.

KLM's legendary social media customer service is provided by a team that handles customers only in those venues. Telephone and e-mail inquiries are fielded by a wholly separate team. According to Karlijn Vogel-Meijer, who leads the social team at KLM, "We really believe that social is different from other channels. You can be really good at the phone, but on social, you have to be good at phrasing things in short sentences. In Twitter, you have only a limited number of characters and you have to solve somebody's problem within that limit, so we need specific skills."

Indeed. Being great at hugging haters on the phone isn't quite the same as doing so in social media. But is it worth it to design your customer service program that way if one of the corresponding results is that data aren't unified and consumers are frustrated? (Note, that's not the case for KLM, where they have a strong data unification program.)

The second issue—software not configured to handle all the new channels alongside the old ones—is harder to fix, although companies like Aspect, Salesforce, Parature, Thunderhead, HP, and Clarabridge are working hard to make seamless. But it's a complex problem rooted in the fact that databases are designed to have a "master" record that identifies each customer. In today's offstage plus onstage world, picking a venue to be the master is far less obvious than it used to be.

"The problem is not lack of data, because we collect the data," says Esteban Kolsky. "The problem is that we don't have a common data model or repository where all this data is accumulated. So if you come to Facebook and I collect your data, I put it in a database where the phone agent cannot access it. Or even if they can access it, they don't understand it because it has a different format than they're used to or has the information that is different from what they know. So this inconsistency is the lack of a common data model. . . . If you look at the way software platforms handle data, there's a very common model; for example, there's a common customer ID number, and there's a common problem and there's a common solution field and things like that. The old systems, they all have their own different ways to manage this. When you want to bring the old systems into the modern cloud, you need to be able to accommodate the model so that it runs in the cloud."

Facebook, Twitter, and the other social media platforms have their own data models that are less than perfectly compatible with legacy systems. Review sites like Yelp and TripAdvisor and Dealer-Rater and the rest are even less suited, at least today, to push and pull data seamlessly. This is why something seemingly simple like Debbie Goldberg tracking Yelp reviews and gift cards sent may be easier to do by hand in a separate system than it is inside a full-fledged customer service software package.

Customers are clear in their overwhelming preference for data unification. Find a way to start moving down this path. You may need to reconfigure your customer service team structure. You may need to rewire how data are captured, stored, and accessed. You may need to do both.

And Resolve the Issue

One of the tenets of modern marketing and customer service is to listen. It's an axiom so common that it's lost all prescriptive power at this point. It also doesn't go nearly far enough. Yes, you should listen to your customers, but it's far more important to actually resolve their issues, not just hear them.

The people handling offstage haters must have the capability and power to actually do something that puts the complaint to rest for the customer. Anything else is just kicking the can down the curb, wasting time, and making customers angry.

There are two reasons why people answering calls or replying to e-mails can't actually resolve the issues surfaced by the customer.

The first reason is that customer service personnel don't know *how* to solve the problem. This can be fixed. Collect and analyze all complaints and problems (consider printing e-mails and transcribing telephone calls). Software from Clarabridge and others make this work seamlessly for big companies. Then use team meetings and rehearsal exercises so that everyone who interacts with customers understands precisely how to solve all common (and even uncommon) customer issues.

People interacting with customers need to know as much or more about the business as team members in any other corner of the company. This is why the concept that the way to staff customer service is with low-paid, low-skill, replaceable employees is self-defeating at the maximum level.

And while this chapter is about the playbook for hugging offstage haters, staffing customer service incorrectly is perhaps even more problematic in onstage channels. There is a pervasive belief in many businesses that the people interacting with customers on Facebook, Twitter, and the like should always be quite young because they "grew up with this stuff" and are comfortable with the technology. It makes sense only if those young people are also quite experienced in the company and its culture. If they always have to ask someone else how to address a particular customer issue, what you gain in technology aptitude you lose in slow response time. It's easier to teach someone Twitter than it is to teach someone your entire business.

Ultimately, for great customer service interactions, it's about understanding. As Lee Cockerell writes in *The Customer Rules*, "Knowledge is power, and a knowledgeable employee can turn a vaguely interested consumer into a purchasing customer and a one-time customer into a regular customer. We all know how frustrating it is to do business with ill-informed employees."[8]

The second reason customer complaints aren't resolved is that the business doesn't feel they deserve to be fully addressed. This is often an outgrowth of a culture that doesn't value the customer experience.

Melinda Masse experienced this at a popular restaurant near her home in Texas. As she relayed to Peter Shankman in his book *Zombie Loyalists*, she had ordered a dessert and the manager asked if perhaps she'd rather have a different one. She didn't. That's when the manager told her they didn't have what she wanted but they would "make it up to [her] next time." This happened on Melinda's next two trips to the restaurant as well; she ordered the dessert (and was even told it was available), only to have the manager tell her they actually didn't have what she wanted but he would "make it up to her next time." Though she was listened to, her problem was never actually successfully addressed.

As Melinda recalled, "I haven't been back since, and you know what the worst part is? I would have been happy if he'd just said 'I'm sorry' and then given me either a modest discount or not charged me for the cheap glass of wine I'd been drinking. But they never wanted to do anything in the present; it was always 'next time.'"

You can't just acknowledge customer complaints, because by answering at all you create an expectation of resolution. Then, when you don't solve the problem, it creates a whole new wave of customer disappointment, just like it did for Melinda. If you answer, be prepared to take the interaction with customers all the way to the finish line.

With Speed

It may seem unusual to be recommending quick issue resolution in an offstage playbook. After all, customer expectations for response times are lower for telephone and e-mail inquiries, compared to social media and other onstage channels. But replying to customer complaints in social media quickly is essentially a given. No business with even a modicum of understanding of those venues would argue that it should answer Facebook posts "when they get around to it." Rapidity is in the DNA of social media.

But for legacy, offstage venues, the helix is quite different. Some businesses take advantage of the comparatively sluggish pace of these channels, stretch out their response times, and imperil their customer relationships as a result.

As we discussed in chapter 3, 67 percent of haters who complain by telephone are satisfied with response time. Only 61 percent of haters are satisfied with e-mail response time, and it's perhaps remarkable that it's even that high given that the average time taken to answer queries submitted via e-mail has increased by a whopping eight hours since 2014 to just short of forty-four hours.[9]

Forty-four hours—nearly two days—for an e-mail reply? No wonder more and more customers are opting to use onstage channels instead, taking previously private exchanges and making them public.

Speed matters, even in channels not known to be speedy. In fact, research from Parature shows that more than four in ten consumers say speed is the most important aspect of a good customer service experience.[10]

Wade Lombard from Square Cow Movers drills his team on the importance of speed, online and offline. "If we're talking about negative stuff, we do have a set response time, and that's immediately," he said. "I literally trained my managers 'Stop what you're doing right then and deal with it right that second.' And if we're still on a job, and we get a call from an unhappy client, and our guys are still there on the job, our managers know that the rule is 'Stop what

Most Important Elements of a Good Customer Experience

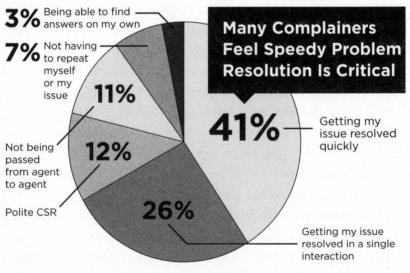

3% Being able to find answers on my own

7% Not having to repeat myself or my issue

11%

Not being passed from agent to agent

Polite CSR

12%

Many Complainers Feel Speedy Problem Resolution Is Critical

41% Getting my issue resolved quickly

26% Getting my issue resolved in a single interaction

Parature, 2014

you're doing, get up, go get in your car, drive to the job, and you're going to stay on that job until the job's done.' We don't waste one second because we think when things linger, when people have time to marinate on them and you don't respond, it just gets worse. It never gets better."

To Lombard, a forty-four-hour response time on e-mail would be unthinkable. "This morning we actually had someone e-mail us and say, 'Hey, I think I was charged sixty dollars for some materials that I didn't actually need.' And the guy was obviously not upset, he was just trying to find a solution. And so I e-mailed a manager who would handle that, and he was busy on the phone. I didn't hear from him for like fifteen minutes. And fifteen minutes for me is like a year. And so I called him, like, 'Hey, did you get my e-mail?' and he was like, 'Yeah, but I was the phone. I'm going to jump on this right now.' So we jump on things immediately. We don't let them linger, ever," he says.

Dan Gingiss, formerly of Discover, finds it amazing that so many companies are trying to get fast at social media customer service with no demonstrated ability to be equally nimble in offstage channels. "Before you try to do customer service in social media, you've got to be good at customer service in other channels," he says. "If you don't have the service culture that we have, you're going to likely get killed in social media. The idea that you would wait hours or days to respond to somebody wouldn't fly in any other channel. It would be akin to letting the phone ring off the hook."

Right now, offstage haters still represent the majority of all complainers. For you, they might even be the overwhelming majority. Remember as well that this group is likely to be slightly older than other customers, and thus may represent a disproportionate share of total customer value.

Offstage haters aren't out in the open, so it's easier to delay responses and treat them as an obligation, not an opportunity. But one of the key lessons of *Hug Your Haters* is that when you disappoint these offstage haters, they move the interaction to public, onstage venues where it can become even more difficult to satisfy them. So embrace these offstage customers while they are still doing you the favor of complaining in private. Just remember: H-O-U-R-S.

Be Human
Use One Channel
Unify Your Data
and Resolve the Issue
with Speed

For even more detailed training on how to hug offstage haters, visit HugYourHaters.com, where you'll find webinars, community discussions, and more.

Chapter 7

F-E-A-R-S: The Playbook for
Hugging Onstage Haters

Dealing with haters in onstage channels can, of course, be tricky. There are many venues for complaints—and more all the time, including WhatsApp, WeChat, dedicated customer service apps, and more.

There's also an increasing volume of negativity. And there's a belief that if companies are going to respond and reply online, they should do so quickly. But the complexity of onstage channels isn't necessarily what trips you up; it's the absence of a framework you can follow to avoid missteps.

Caught in a maelstrom of customer questions and real-time uncertainty, the Indianapolis Motor Speedway could have used such a playbook.

Torrential rains washed out the first day of driver qualifying for the 2015 edition of the Indianapolis 500, the largest and most famous automobile race in the United States. When the cancellation was announced after just a few cars had tried to qualify in a pretorrent mist, many ticket holders went to social media to ask about refunds.

Drew Hester asked on Twitter:

> @IMS *since qualifying is rained out can tickets purchased today be used as a rain check tomorrow*[1]

The racetrack replied, but they did so with a startling lack of compassion and nuance:

> @drewhester12 *Today's tickets will not be honored to-morrow.*[2]

The speedway sent similar replies to many customers on Twitter, and posted fundamentally the same message on Facebook: no refunds. The outcry was swift, both about the lack of refunds for an event that had essentially not taken place and especially for the unsympathetic and abrupt social media replies from the track.

Eventually, the IMS yielded, and tickets were made valid for the following day's successful, rain-free qualifying.

Answering onstage haters quickly and appropriately is viable, as we've seen throughout this book, with case studies and examples of companies of every size and many types.

Here's the playbook the IMS evidently didn't have: the formula for hugging onstage haters. To make it easier to remember, I've created a mnemonic, similar to the offstage hater playbook. For onstage haters, the key lessons to remember are F-E-A-R-S:

Find All Mentions

Display **E**mpathy

Answer Publicly

Reply Only Twice

Switch Channels

You may notice that I didn't include "be fast" as a specific component of the onstage haters' playbook. This is because it is axiomatic. As we discovered in chapter 3, nearly 40 percent of all social media complainers who anticipate a response expect it to arrive within sixty minutes. Yet the average length of time for businesses to actually respond is five hours. Closing that gap is critical, and should be a focus for any legitimate online customer service program.

Find All Mentions

It's impossible to hug the haters you never see. In the legacy, offstage channels of phone and telephone, this isn't an issue. If someone calls your business, you know they called. The phone was either answered or the caller left a message. (If you do not have voice mail at this point, put down this book and get that sorted out. I'll wait for you.) The same is true for e-mail; there's no detective work needed to find them, they just show up on your computer, phone, or tablet.

But with the proliferation of onstage channels, it's entirely possible—likely, even—that you are oblivious to customer complaints being logged at this moment. Ignorance can be purposeful: several of my friends own businesses and they completely ignore review sites, assuming, incorrectly, as we've seen, that Yelp and the like aren't worth the effort. But most of the time, not finding all of your online customer feedback means you simply lack sufficient vigor in your search.

At the basic level, all companies should be using a combination of Google alerts and simple social media listening software. Even free versions from Mention.net and Hootsuite may be enough for small businesses. You need to find public, online references to your company and your products or services. Most mentions of your business in discussion boards and forums will show up in Google, but it may take a while. If there are particular forums where your business is more likely to be referenced, and there almost assuredly are, manually review them every day or two and check for mentions. The same is true for review sites like Yelp, TripAdvisor, Spiceworks, or any of the hundreds of industry-specific rating platforms. If you're a plastic surgeon, someone in your office should be looking at RealSelf every day, forever.

At the next level, companies should consider software that finds mentions across many venues and rolls them together in a unified dashboard that functions similar to an e-mail inbox, but includes tweets, Facebook posts, Angie's List reviews, and the like. These software packages can be real time savers, especially for small businesses that do not have personnel devoted entirely to customer service. Yext is one such package, and also helps with local search engine optimization. ReviewTrackers is another strong option.

For bigger companies, dedicated listening/response software like Sprout Social, NewBrand, Conversocial, and Lithium are often required to monitor and locate as many mentions as possible, across a wide swath of channels. This is especially important for businesses that have many physical locations, as the listening function is usually performed by a central team, which then distributes key mentions to each location as warranted.

"Through NewBrand, we have a daily alert system, so every morning all the location operators get all reviews from the past twenty-four hours, in all the different channels, sent to their e-mail," says Erin Pepper of Le Pain Quotidien.

Another reason software is a useful tool in the quest to find all customer feedback is that much of that feedback doesn't mention the company specifically. Remember, a little less than half of the onstage haters are expecting to hear back from the company, so in many cases they do not phrase their complaints in an obvious way that ties it back to the business.

Conversocial partnered with New York University on research that found that more than one-third of all tweets to companies were about customer service issues, but only 3 percent incorporated the company's Twitter username with the @ symbol. This means that many mentions of your business online—on Twitter and beyond— may be indirect, which is why it's crucial that you have a system that catches those complaints and comments.[3]

A new type of software has recently emerged that takes a different approach to the same problem. While most listening software helps you deploy an array of keywords to locate indirect and non-obvious complaints, they find comments and complaints that include only those keywords. But what if the complaint doesn't mention you at all, directly or indirectly? Software from Geofeedia bridges that gap.

Instead of using keywords to find commentary, Geofeedia uses location. Draw a circle, square, or any other shape around a geographic area and Geofeedia will show you all the geotagged social media content posted from within that region. Turning geotagging on so that location is digitally attached to the tweet, Facebook post, Instagram upload, or other form of commentary is a standard part of most social platforms; Geofeedia estimates that approximately 15 percent of all social content includes geotags. Businesses with a physical location (or several, like all the franchise locations in a state) are now using the platform to locate comments and content that previously would have been invisible.

Clearly, you should commit to answering direct customer complaints and questions first. Then, once you have a good system in place for hugging those haters, expanding your net and addressing a larger share of indirect complaints is the best next step—and one that's easier to do with increasingly sophisticated technology.

Display Empathy

Though onstage haters may not expect a reply, they definitely desire an audience. That's why they raise the stakes and take grievances to a public forum. They want onlookers to chime in with variations on the theme of "I'm appalled! How dare they treat you this way!" Their complaints are often filled with language that vacillates between colorful and outrageous. It creates the reaction they seek, from the audience and possibly from you. They are angry. They write something scathing and post it online. Now you're angry, too.

When you read a highly negative review about your business, you not only feel angry but experience a very real physical reaction, according to a journal article titled "Physiology of Anger": "As you become angry your body's muscles tense up. Inside your brain, neurotransmitter chemicals known as catecholamines are released causing you to experience a burst of energy lasting up to several minutes. This burst of energy is behind the common angry desire to take immediate protective action. At the same time your heart rate accelerates, your blood pressure rises, and your rate of breathing increases. You're now ready to fight."[4]

Accelerated heart rate. Increased blood pressure. Rapid breathing. These are not the ideal conditions for a speedy, empathetic response to customer complaints. But you have to find a way to keep your cool in the face of haters, or find the people in your business who can do so. Engaging in a sequence of acrimonious accusations with customers in a public, online forum never works. The business is never the perceived victor, even if it was truly in the right. Yet back-and-forth "flame wars" are not rare. They happen a lot, and they happen because the person answering customer complaints is unable to put empathy for the customer ahead of her physiological desire to fight.

"Just have a human interaction with that person, even if it is online," says Matt Gentile of Century 21. "Do it in such a way that lets them know that you are listening, you've heard their complaint, you're taking actions to investigate their complaint, and then follow up on whatever the results of that investigation were, one way or the other. I think you'll find that greatly reduces the intensity of the interaction."

Inserting empathy into your interactions with onstage haters doesn't mean that you give them all wet, sloppy kisses. It doesn't mean you bend over backward. It doesn't mean the customer is always right. It does mean the customer is always heard, and you should acknowledge, instantly and often, that the person is having a problem that your business likely caused somehow. A short "I'm sorry" goes a long, long way.

My friend Chris Rund is a graphic designer, cat owner, and onstage hater. A year ago, he left a message on the Facebook page of Meow Mix, a popular brand of cat food in the United States. Chris said:

> *Dear Meow Mix,*
>
> *Cats throw up. Pretty regularly. (I figured you guys would realize this, being cat experts and all.) With this in mind, why do you insist on putting dyes in your product that cause ruined carpets, furniture, etc. when kitty spews her half-digested Meow yuck all over? Seriously, my cat doesn't give a Sh*t what your product looks like in a bowl, and neither do I. What would be helpful and appreciated (by legions of cat owners, I'm guessing) is if you'd take the worthless dyes out of your product and save us all a lot of frustration and ruined fabrics.*

To their credit, Meow Mix responded. They did so in public, and they did it relatively fast, within twenty-four hours. What they didn't do was deploy empathy. They didn't say they were sorry for Chris's ruined fabrics or about his cat's tendency toward reversals of fortune at mealtimes. They just used the standard corporate line that deflects blame in a robotic way that is the opposite of helpful and a far cry from satisfying. They hugged their hater, but they didn't mean it. Meow Mix replied:

> *Hi Chris. All Meow Mix products are made with nutri-tious, quality ingredients that meet the standards and specifi-cations of the U.S. Department of Agriculture (USDA), Association of American Feed Control Officials (AAFCO) and the Food and Drug Administration (FDA). If you have further questions, our consumer affairs team will be able to help you. You can reach them at 1-877-MEOW-MIX (877-636-9649) or by visiting meowmix.com and clicking the "Contact Us" link at the bottom of the page.*

This is not empathy, this is copy and paste. As if dropping the acronym for the almighty American Feed Control Officials is a universal salve. If your customer service personnel, especially online, have any responses in their quiver of standard answers that read like this, find them and start over. Because in some cases, scripted, tone-deaf responses are as bad as no response at all.

Sarah Maloy from Shutterstock has a secret for avoiding this trap: "Think about how you would want to be spoken to in the same situation," she says. "It's all about being understanding. Allow yourself to have a voice and allow your brand to have a personality. And don't get locked down by prewritten approved language."

Answer Publicly

While Meow Mix's response didn't fully, or even partially, address Chris's question, at least it replied publicly. Doing so is an important part of the playbook for handling onstage haters.

Remember, online customer service is a spectator sport. Sure, you want to make the hater happy, but the opinions of the onlookers are the bigger prize. Whether you're in apology mode or responding to a positive comment, if your customer is choosing to interact with you in public, respond in the same way, at least at first. If you respond in private, you are squandering the trust capital gained by being open and transparent in how you handle customer feedback.

Tim Handorf is the cofounder of G2 Crowd, a platform for ratings and reviews of B2B software, and he believes in the power of being public. "I would start with being honest and transparent in all cases," he says. "So if you make a mistake, I would admit to it and I would then focus on what you're doing to handle it and why it wouldn't occur again. I think transparency is the key. Transparency in my opinion is equal to trust, and in today's world of social media and what I call 'everyone's naked,' you've got to have it."

You might think, "Well, who cares if they leave us a G2 Crowd review and we reply back to them with a private message? At least we're replying!" First, the spectators on G2 Crowd don't know you replied. Second, that kind of channel switching on the first response can be confusing for the customer. Imagine if the equation was reversed. What if someone left you a voice mail, and you then tweeted them, "@Jaybaer Thanks for the voice mail. How can I help you?" That crosses the line from responsive to creepy.

Don't be afraid of the technology limits of onstage channels either. Indeed, it can seem like a restriction to have only 140 characters to respond on Twitter or to follow sometimes arcane guidelines when crafting a reply in a discussion board or forum. But this is where you can apply creativity to your responses. This is where the commitment to burning the script and empowering your customer service personnel to add empathy and humanity pays off in surprise and delight.

My friend Scott Stratten is a fantastic keynote speaker and author of many books, including *QR Codes Kill Kittens*. He's a tech-savvy guy who spends an unhealthy amount of time on Twitter. Consequently, when the streaming music service Spotify launched in Canada (Scott lives outside Toronto), he complained on Twitter first. Scott is an onstage hater.

In truth, his "complaint" was more of an observation. He posted:

> *With Spotify being new to Canada, I don't really under-stand how to use it right, but damn, I like it.*[5]

Scott Stratten @unmarketing · Oct 9
With Spotify being new to Canada, I don't really understand how to use it right, but damn, I like it.

🔁 2   ⭐ 13   •••

SpotifyCares ✓
@SpotifyCares   ⚙   +👤 Follow

@unmarketing We're here for you, Scott, take a look at this: spoti.fi/1rl9OyC

TRACK

+ Hey

+ Mr. Scott

+ Welcome to the Party   EXPLICIT

+ We're Here for a Good Time

+ So

+ Don't Worry About a Thing

+ We'll Be Here When You Need Us

+ Just

+ Shout

+ And

+ We

+ Will

+ Come Running

(Notice that Scott mentioned Spotify but didn't specifically include the @Spotify or @SpotifyCares Twitter handles. That's exactly what Conversocial's research found to be the case 97 percent of the time.)

Spotify could have constrained themselves to Twitter's 140-character limit and sent Scott a reply that said something like, "We're sorry you're having trouble. You can find our Frequently Asked Questions here: [insert link]." But they didn't do that. They did so much more.

Spotify replied to Scott on Twitter and included an image capture of a custom music playlist created just for him, where every song title fit together to form a coded message of support. Including a link to the custom playlist as well, the tweet read:

> @unmarketing *We're here for you, Scott, take a look at this: spoti.fi/1rl9OyC*

The songs on the playlist:

Hey
Mr. Scott
Welcome to the Party
We're Here for a Good Time
So
Don't Worry About a Thing
We'll Be Here When You Need Us
Just
Shout
And
We
Will
Come Running[6]

To which Scott tweeted back the only thing he could, really:

@SpotifyCares Now that's awesome.[7]

The fact that Spotify put this together in fourteen hours, at night (Scott tweeted at nine P.M. initially), is amazing. More amazing is that there is a song titled "And" in the Spotify library. (It's by The Telescopes.)

Your customers aren't always just curious and confused like Scott Stratten. Sometimes they are downright angry. Or your hater might be one of the few irate and irrational customers we defined as "the crazies" in chapter 2. Regardless of who the hater is, however, I recommend responding publicly. Even if they rant and rave and call you names, you'll answer coolly and publicly. It probably won't change the behavior or attitude of that one person, as it's almost impossible to turn a crazy lemon into lemonade; the fruit is already rotten. But by replying in public you show your temperament, your values, and your belief that all customers deserve to be heard. (The exceptions to this playbook are when threats are made, especially toward individual employees. At that point, do not reply. Document all communication and contact law enforcement immediately.)

Jordan Pierson, the chief marketing officer at Wink Frozen Desserts, believes censorship and deleting negative posts do more harm than good. "I would recommend not censoring people, because the younger generation is even more savvy to those things," he says. "I know Facebook has a tool that lets you hide a comment on your page from everyone but the person who left it, so when they come back they'll still see the comment and have the impression that they haven't been censored, while the rest of the Facebook audience won't see it at all. But I just think that the younger generation will figure those things out. So you're better off trying to handle the situation rationally using information than to just try to shush them and get them out of the room."

Reply Only Twice

This is the question I get most often about the Hug Your Haters system: "What if I respond to a hater, and he replies back with something even more negative?"

It happens all the time. Onstage haters see you respond and believe they have a foil, an opponent, a punching bag. But they do not. Because you and your customer service personnel know the key to effective onstage interactions: Jay Baer's Rule of Reply Only Twice.

My Rule of Reply Only Twice is simple, and developed and proven across my twenty-two years as an online marketing and customer experience consultant. The rule is:

Online, never reply more than twice to any one person in any single conversation.

Violating the Rule of Reply Only Twice can drag you down into a vortex of negativity and hostility, and it's also a waste of your time. Here's how it works in practice. We'll use a fictional hater called "Chad" (just a coincidence and not in any way related to the kid of the same name who tormented me in high school).

> **Chad:** You guys are the absolute worst. I can't believe you actually have the guts to accept American currency for your terrible product!
>
> **Business:** We seem to have fallen short in your eyes, Chad. Can you tell me more about what happened, and I'll do whatever I can to assist?
>
> **Chad:** It won't matter. It's not like an idiot like you can fix all that's wrong with this ridiculous company.
>
> **Business:** I'm sorry you're unhappy, and would like to help if possible. Please contact me via private message if you'd like me to give it a try.

At this point, if Chad continues to complain, just let him do so. You've made two legitimate attempts to solve his problem. He has acknowledged this to be true by replying back to you, and the spectators will see the same. Now it's time to let it go and walk away.

Nothing will be gained by replying again and again. You've done your part. You're on record. Move on.

The Rule of Reply Only Twice does not dictate that you always have to answer twice, just that you never answer more than twice. One reply is sufficient for the majority of hater scenarios.

Ironically, even though customer interactions usually happen more quickly in onstage venues than offstage venues like e-mail, it is important that you not respond instantly in social media, review sites, or forums. Quickly? Yes. Instantly? No. Instant replies are dangerous, as you can get caught up in the anger maelstrom and respond in a manner that is less than optimal.

Wade Lombard at Square Cow Movers has an internal pause policy with regard to public, online replies. "We have this rule that you need to stop, and you need to just wait a little while," he says. "Because when you respond, realize you're not responding just to this person, you're responding to all of earth, and so make sure that you're responding in a way that when folks read it, regardless of the circumstances, they're reading something from the business that reads well and it reads respectfully."

Switch Channels

In the H-O-U-R-S playbook for handling offstage haters, I recommended that you avoid switching channels, and instead endeavor mightily to solve customers' problems within the venue they have selected as their preferred contact mechanism. This is not the case when working with onstage haters, for two reasons.

First, the truncated nature of many onstage channels means it may be impossible to fully address a complex complaint in only two interactions. Second, you may need the customer's account number or other sensitive details to assist him, and you should not ask him to expose that information in full view of the digital spectators.

So for nuanced customer interactions that require research to resolve, your goal should be to switch channels after your initial, public response.

More than 60 percent of businesses say they are not capable of handling customer issues in one contact in social media.[8] Many inquiries through these channels involve at least a second contact, in which the customer is sent to the telephone channel for resolution. This increases company costs, as they are adding a pricey telephone call on top of a comparatively inexpensive social media interaction. In this common scenario, customers who have chosen to be onstage haters are now forced to move back offstage.

For the tech-savvy customer segment (like Scott Stratten) that uses public channels not because they have been disappointed with legacy customer support but because they simply prefer it (it's their natural habitat), asking them to dial the phone to follow up on a tweet is like instructing them to churn their own butter to solve a problem with bland mashed potatoes.

A better method is that whenever you need to take a public, onstage customer interaction private, do so in the hidden chambers of the original contact channel. Fortunately, almost all onstage channels offer this functionality to businesses. Take advantage of it.

If a hater reaches out to your business on Twitter and you need her account number to investigate, in your first reply apologize and ask her to send a direct message with her account number. Twitter has changed its policy on direct, private messages so that communicants don't have to "follow" each other to use this feature. This is a meaningful enhancement, as it eliminates the need for a company to ask an irate customer to first follow the business before she can send a direct message. A follow is customarily a signal of support and positivity, the opposite of a complaint. The previous system was often awkward, the digital equivalent of "Put a bumper sticker on your car in support of me, and then send me a letter telling me how much you hate me."

You can use direct messages on Facebook, as well as on most review sites; Erin Pepper from Le Pain Quotidien uses the Yelp private message system to recruit haters to become her secret shoppers. Nearly every discussion board and forum has a private message feature as well, an option many companies are using regularly.

Customer Hank Strickland left this comment on the Facebook page of Manitoba Telecom Services in 2015:

> *Hey MTS. Your picture messaging has been having problems for a long time now. Anytime I call MTS they say they are working on it. My contract is almost done and I definitely will not be re-signing with MTS.*[9]

MTS replied appropriately, combining a public response with a request to move the conversation to the parallel, private version of the channel:

> *Hi Hank, we're really sorry to hear that. If you are considering keeping your device after the contract is up we would definitely love to help assist you to get that working. Feel free to send us a private message with your phone number and we'll look into it today.*[10]

Strickland then added several other replies, none productive. The MTS customer service team handled these missives by ignoring them. They perhaps could have replied a second time (but no more than that, per the Rule of Replying Only Twice). They offered a viable channel switch, and the customer refused to accept that offer.

Compare that approach to this exchange on the Facebook page of Subway restaurants, where customer Jeff Hunt left this comment under a photo of a sandwich posted by the brand in May 2015:

> *Never ever looks like that. Employees at local subways are super lazy . . . half the time my sandwich falls out and dressing gets all over my shirt and shorts/pants. I've ruined at least three very expensive dress shirts already due to them.*[11]

Subway replied in public and asked for the channel switch, but to do what the company asked put all the onus and effort on the customer:

> *Thanks for writing Jeff. We regret that you were disappointed with your experience at this Subway location, and we would like to contact the local owner to address the issues you brought to our attention. If you could kindly link directly to our Customer Care team at http://bit.ly/bhSAn and share the details including the specific location and your contact information, we can contact the local store owner and he will contact you directly. We're really glad you took the time to let us know about your Subway experience and give us a chance to make this right for you.*[12]

On a computer, clicking the link provided by Subway will take the customer to an online form that is stark, confusing, and limits comments to three thousand characters, an imperfect next step in the process of hugging this hater. But it's far better than what happens if the link is clicked on a mobile device. In that very common circumstance, the customer is redirected to the Subway home page, complete with an ad for the sandwiches that caused the original complaint! That's a poor customer experience in general, but it's exacerbated by the fact that 526 million people worldwide use Facebook only on a mobile device as of January 2015.[13] Half a billion people not able to access your publicly displayed complaint form may be an issue worth examining.

Conversely, some businesses switch from public to private channels and use the transition to build humanity and empathy. Twitter, in particular, is a current leader in this opportunity as the platform has enabled businesses and consumers to create and send short videos instead of text and photos. Interacting with haters through video can have a positive psychological effect, according to Michael Maoz from Gartner: "When a customer looks at a customer support person on-screen, their heart rate goes down, their blood pressure goes down, their euphoria goes up. Why? It's really much more difficult to fail to be empathetic with a human being who is looking at you. The customer doesn't have to be seen, but the fact that the customer support person is on-screen, it's a lot harder for me to be nasty in that situation."

Prescription eyeglasses manufacturer Warby Parker embraces this opportunity in full, public view. Its customer service team selects tweets and Facebook messages from customers and creates video replies. These videos are posted on YouTube and the link is sent to the customer in social media. During the 2014 holiday season, customer Whitney Fowler tweeted a photo of herself wearing a pair of Warby Parker eyeglass frames she was considering for a purchase:

> @WarbyParkerHelp *What do yall think? Any recommendations?*[14]

The business could have easily replied with "They look great, Whitney! Nice choice!" But instead, they took it to an entirely new level. Cue the surprise and delight as a Warby Parker representative

Whitney Fowler
@whitlash

@WarbyParkerHelp What do yall think? Any recommendations?

Warby Parker | We Really Love Your Welty Frames

wrote a custom, seasonal jingle for Whitney, posted it to YouTube, and then tweeted her the link.[15]

Wow! Now, that's making the most of a channel switch. Warby Parker makes these videos typically when customers are asking for advice, not complaining.

JetBlue airlines will switch channels in a negative situation, and completely shock consumers as a result. It happened last year to Tom Webster, who directed the research we conducted for *Hug Your Haters* and wrote the foreword to this book.

Tom is a frequent JetBlue flier and knows how airplanes are supposed to sound and feel. Flying from Boston to Charlotte in an exit row seat next to the window, he heard an unusual grinding noise early in the flight, and noticed the fuselage becoming steadily warmer. The aircraft was hot to the touch throughout most of the flight, and Webster was understandably concerned. Flight attendants were informed but were noncommittal about what they would do about it, and couldn't do much in the air anyway. Upon landing, Webster tweeted the airline and reported the incident.

JetBlue's Laurie Meacham, manager of customer commitment, remembers Webster's tweet.

"I do remember that, actually. And it's a great example because it's not like we did it just because of who he is," Meacham recalls. "It is something that's pretty typical of what we do with anybody. So obviously that's a pretty big concern and that's an issue, when the plane is so hot. And my team noticed it. They raised the flag, like, 'Hey, this sounds concerning. What's going on?' And from there it's just a series of: Who do we need to talk to? How can we find out what's going on? Let's close the loop. I know we involved a member of our technical operations team to try to troubleshoot the issue."

JetBlue didn't just tweet Webster back or ask him to engage in a series of private, direct messages. Instead, the company publicly tweeted that they would look into it, but then switched channels proactively. Within hours, Tom received an inbound telephone call, on his cell phone, from a senior JetBlue operations representative.

"I was amazed," he says. "Somehow they had seen my tweet and then figured out what flight I was on, as I didn't mention it originally. Then they found my cell phone number. And then had someone call me personally. The coordination of all that is staggering to consider."

Meacham explains how the detective work was accomplished: "Even though his Twitter handle is pretty cryptic [@webby2001], the name Tom Webster is something we can search for in our system. We can find a reservation. If he has a TrueBlue account [the JetBlue frequent flier program], we can get his phone number from that, or we can get an e-mail address. Of course, first and foremost we wanted to reach out to him for his sake. But second, we were genuinely curious, like, what is going on and what other information do we need to fix this? And he might have some information that could help us as well."

Evidently, Webster experienced an acute case of a long-standing issue: overheating of the control box that powers the live television available on all JetBlue flights. According to Meacham, all the old units have been replaced.

We've seen what onstage haters expect, and how you can meet and exceed those desires with the F-E-A-R-S playbook. Remember, it's:

Find All Mentions
Display Empathy
Answer Publicly
Reply Only Twice
Switch Channels

We've also examined some of the changes to social media and review sites that enable private messages and effective channel switching.

But those technology advances are just the beginning of the next phase of customer service. What we know about how customer service and customer experience works is about to be disrupted on a massive scale.

Let's look at the future—and in some cases the cutting-edge present—of hugging your haters.

Chapter 8

The Future of Customer Service

Technology adoption and consumer behavior shifts have already changed customer service forever. The simultaneous rise of mobile computing and social media has increased complaint volume and channel breadth. This requires a complete overhaul of how we think about interacting with customers.

We know that haters aren't your problem, ignoring them is. We've learned about the critical differences between offstage and onstage haters, and their respective expectations. But the disruption is far from over, and may never end. Here are five other emerging trends in customer service that will impact how you hug your haters in every channel, every time.

Proactive Customer Experience

While answering onstage complaints is less expensive than legacy contact mechanisms like telephone and e-mail, the costs are real and the public nature of these customer interactions increases risk, even when following the F-E-A-R-S blueprint. So perhaps the best way to invest your resources is to legitimately improve your customer experience so that fewer people have any reason to complain.

If you're paying attention to the insights your haters provide in every complaint, you probably know the weak parts of your business. You know where and when customer satisfaction is likely to dip. So instead of waiting for people to complain, find a way to proactively head them off at the pass. The best way to handle complaints is to eliminate them.

This doesn't mean you make it harder to complain, like Subway customers using Facebook on a mobile phone. It means using what you know and what consumers tell you to improve your business and reaching out proactively in circumstances where a complaint may be forthcoming. Nowhere is it written that the customer has to make the first move. Contact them before they contact you, and watch their customer advocacy soar!

"Better communication along the customer journey is a major missed opportunity," claims Michael Allense, senior strategic consulting director at MaritzCX. "It is not just about fixing problems or being there when the customer expresses a need, but it is also being proactive throughout the customer journey. This requires companies to get away from a transactional customer service and customer experience mentality that is more inwardly focused on operations and shift to a customer journey-focused mentality that is centered on the customers' needs and the relationship as a whole."

Debbie Goldberg at Fresh Brothers Pizza lives this proactive principle. "Sometimes we look at our delivery times, and if we are delivering five to ten minutes later than what we quoted the customer, we automatically send gift certificates to those people. It might be a coupon code for 15 percent off next time, or it might be a ten-dollar gift certificate," she says. "It really surprises people. Because sometimes they didn't even think there was an issue, but we knew it was going to be an issue."

The ability to predict a complaint or problem and solve it before patrons notice is customer experience sorcery of the very best kind.

KLM Royal Dutch Airlines has mastered this magic, and in a very complex and fast-moving environment at Amsterdam's Schiphol international airport.

"People lose stuff on planes," says Karlijn Vogel-Meijer, global director of social media at KLM. "Usually, they put their iPads in a seat pocket or something like that. They forget about it, they run off the plane, and then, suddenly, their iPad is lost. What they usually do is they tweet or post and they say, 'Okay, my iPad was in seat pocket 2D on this flight, going to this destination. Have you found it?'"

According to Vogel-Meijer, the airline's procedure used to be that fliers had to visit the company website and submit a lost items form. Then, after five days, customers could call KLM to see if the item had been found. It's a common, albeit clunky, process used by many airlines.

Most of the items lost on a plane are quickly found by the flight attendant and cleaning crews as they prepare for the next flight. They used to take found items to the KLM transfer desk with a note that said, "This was found in seat 2D," and hopefully the airline could match it up with the online forms a few days later. Amsterdam, however, is a major stopover on trans-Europe and other flight paths, and many fliers who forget personal belongings on the plane are still in the airport waiting for their connecting flights when their items are found by the crew.

A member of Vogel-Meijer's social media team who works at the airport found a better way to reconnect customers with their lost items. Armed with only a tablet computer and a smartphone, she completely changed customer service from reactive to proactive.

Without a committee meeting or official policy change—the KLM culture emphasizes employee initiatives—she asked flight crews to call her instead of taking found items to a transfer desk. On her tablet, she could then look up a customer's itinerary and discover that his next flight was leaving from gate 37 to Paris in forty-five minutes.

"She rushes immediately to the gate, looks for Mr. Jensen, and tells him, 'Could it be that you lost something?' Mostly, they don't even know they have lost it yet, and suddenly they have their iPad back," explains Vogel-Meijer.

This proactive program has been so successful, it's expanded to an entire team at Schiphol airport, staffed mostly by flight-crew members who are unable to fly due to pregnancy or other factors. They work temporarily in this real-time lost-and-found center, connecting items with their owners.

Today this predictive approach is remarkable and extraordinary. But your customers will expect it from you in as few as five years from now. According to research from Walker, "The customer of 2020 will be more informed and in charge of the experience they receive. They will expect companies to know their individual needs and personalize the experience. Immediate resolution will not be fast enough as customers will expect companies to proactively address their current and future needs."[1]

Self-Service Solutions

If customers can easily and thoroughly address their problems on their own, they will seek to do so. Self-service is always the most efficient path to resolution, because customers don't have to wait on your business to respond. As Gartner's Michael Maoz says, "The best phone call is the one that didn't happen."

According to Kate Leggett, principal analyst at Forrester Research, self-service increases customer satisfaction and lowers costs for the business.[2] So it makes a lot of sense, on both the customer experience and cost efficiency fronts, to mine your complaints and feedback for patterns and commonalities, and then address those issues with easy-to-access online information.

Customers love this. Forrester found that 72 percent of consumers prefer using a company's website to answer their questions.[3] But businesses are not universally adept at this self-service approach, as only half of customers can find the information they need online.[4]

The best self-service programs are living organisms. They expand and morph to fit changing customer complaints and questions. To do so requires managers to meet often with personnel interacting with customers in other channels, to discuss what new questions and issues are emerging. Analyzing what visitors type into the search function of your website also provides good clues.

Of course, many of the questions are repeats. According to Rahul Sachdev from Get Satisfaction, approximately one-third of customer questions are repeat or common issues. The objective with self-service is to determine all of those likely customer questions, and then provide answers to them, ideally in multiple online formats— text, video, audio, photographs, infographics, and beyond.

Frank Eliason praises Amazon for its devotion to this approach: "Amazon has a model where they believe that if you have to contact us, our website is screwed up and we need to fix it. They try to ensure that no question is asked twice," he says. "Two of the things that companies need to get much better at are taking feedback, and then not just addressing the customer's issue, but addressing it for all customers. That is where you get your greatest value. Instead, most companies have the mind-set that customers are bad because they contact you."

Of course, Amazon is a large company, and can devote considerable resources to perfecting the art of self-service information. But small businesses can do the same.

Not far from my new home in Bloomington, Indiana, is Santa Claus, Indiana, home to Holiday World and Splashin' Safari, one of America's best amusement parks. This family-owned and -operated business may have the best self-service approach of any small company anywhere.

Holiday World embraces the premise that no question is unworthy of an answer and that filling information gaps is an important part of customer experience. Dozens of pages on the website are devoted to when to go, where to park, and what to expect. And for every major attraction at the park, the company provides an array of detailed data about the ride—a complete frequently asked questions section about every element of the experience.[5]

"We want to give them as many tools as we can within the website, without being overly complicated, so that the guest has a real good working knowledge of how to have the best possible day at Holiday World when they choose their day of visit," Dan Koch told me when I interviewed him for my book *Youtility*.[6] Koch was formerly president of Holiday World and now runs Splash Adventure in Alabama.

The most important aspect of Koch's description of their information mission is his emphasis on creating the best possible experience on the day of the guest's visit. The focus of the website isn't on selling the attraction, or getting visitors to come back a second day, or selling T-shirts. It's about using information to improve customer experience, which creates loyalty and word of mouth and reduces complaints. And it's working. Of the 1,593 reviews of Holiday World and Splashin' Safari on TripAdvisor, 1,498 have four or five stars.[7]

There is no downside to self-service. As Paula Werne, director of marketing at Holiday World, says, "We've never been told, 'You're giving us too much information.'"[8]

For their part, consumers don't feel self-service gives them a lesser experience. They actually prefer it. Research in 2015 from the Center for Generational Kinetics and Aspect software found that two-thirds of Americans feel good about themselves and the company about which they have questions when they can solve a problem without talking to customer service. In that study, author and consultant Jason Dorsey recommends that all companies take a Holiday World approach to self-service: "Create a self-help video library that is easy to navigate. Start by reviewing the most common questions or challenges that customers bring to you, and then create a simple video that shows how to solve each one. This could be how to set up an online account, how to replace a battery or how to exchange something previously bought. Use very clear names for each video so that customers can type in a specific question and get recommendations that match their query. The key is that the videos should include simple step-by-step instructions and be easily viewed on any mobile device."[9]

Self-service seems like a universally applicable solution to drive down costs while simultaneously increasing customer satisfaction. Why doesn't every company commit to it? According to Joe Gagnon from customer service software provider Aspect, it's because most companies don't fundamentally trust their customers enough to solve problems without intervention from the business. "Amazon has proven it can work," Gagnon says. "Give me more information, show me you believe in me as a customer, and I'll be more loyal. Show me the prices of your competitors. Give me alternative products. Give me both good and critical reviews. It's just like with your children; the more power you give them, the more respect they give back to you."

Gagnon also acknowledges that some companies refuse to adopt self-service because it inherently robs them of the opportunity to combine service with revenue generation (like my casino customer satisfaction survey from chapter 5). "Sometimes the business model gets in the way of self-service because we want to manipulate the outcome. I may want to be able to up-sell you, or cross-sell you," he says.

Community-Based Service

If the most efficient way to get answers to consumers is to allow access to them in a self-service capacity, the next best approach may be to enable support from a robust customer community. Like self-service, providing a mechanism where customers can assist one another can result in significant decreases in contacts and complaints reaching the company.

Esteban Kolsky from thinkJar believes community-based service will continue to grow in importance, because collectively, the community knows more than any one customer service representative possibly could. "Communities will change the way we do everything. Partly it's because the knowledge contained in the community is much more relevant and powerful than the knowledge that you can have pretty much anywhere else. If you actually build a good community and your customers come in and become your support structure within the community, you reduce the number of phone calls. Have your customers answer the questions," says Kolsky.

Community-based service can work, even at large scale. James Degnan from Xbox says 70 to 80 percent of all consumer questions are answered by the community, mostly by official "Ambassadors" who have been sanctioned to do so. When they find an issue they can address in the Xbox discussion boards, they are empowered to jump in and provide a solution. Degnan describes it as a "marriage of forums and peer-to-peer help."

The financial implications of this program are staggering and support findings from Gartner, whose research suggests that companies that implement community-based support can reduce costs by 10 to 50 percent.[10]

Sachdev's Get Satisfaction is a long-standing platform provider that companies use to connect with their customers online through communities. He understands that the community is only as powerful as the advocates who spend their time helping other customers.

One of Get Satisfaction's customers is Canadian mobile phone provider Koodo, a division of Telus. Koodo's business model aims to provide the least expensive cell phone service in Canada while still providing great customer service. Providing exceptional customer service at a rock-bottom price can be mutually exclusive in some cases, as Sachdev explains. "Every time a customer calls you about a question or a problem, that could cost the company between ten and fifty dollars per interaction. And for a business like Koodo, the average revenue per user might only be forty or fifty dollars per month.

So if every customer called you once a month, that would totally destroy the economics of that business," he says.

Koodo launched a Get Satisfaction community support center online called Mobile Masters. Customers designated as "Mobile Masters" are passionate about the company and, like the Xbox Ambassadors, answer most of the questions from other consumers—as many as 99 percent of all inquiries.

"If you were to design a customer support department from scratch today, would you create a one-to-one channel? You wouldn't. You would actually think about something closer to a community. So why don't we do that all the time?" Sachdev asks. "Businesses often have a misperception that high-touch customer care and personalized customer care are needed by everybody. My response is, 'It is certainly needed by some subset of customers, but actually not everybody.' And the new generation actually values convenience, self-help, and community help much more than the older generation, and actually is much more willing to contribute answers, too," he says. "And I think we should just embrace that and redesign customer support processes, starting with community first, and think about telephone and e-mail as the second option, not the first option."

Online communities can also breed deep insights that allow businesses and organizations to change their offerings, communicate more effectively, and enhance customer service when it does need to be provided on a one-to-one basis. Vision Critical is a software platform company that creates and operates these types of insight communities, creating a flow of "collective wisdom" from customers that helps the community owners improve their operations. A recent Vision Critical community in Montreal, Quebec, sought to collect feedback from users of public transportation in advance of a merger of transit lines and methods by the Société de transport de Montréal. More than seven thousand people have participated in the My voice my STM community and the subsequent insights are very useful, according to Société de transport de Montréal marketing director Pierre Bourbonnière. "STM has been able to use the insight community to quickly turn around feedback, target specific types of riders or prospects, and cut costs," he says.[11]

The benefits of community support can transcend reduced customer service expenses and insight generation, and actually create new revenue in the process. That's the premise of Needle, the software and training company that puts your customers to work.

"We find the advocates. For example, Adidas's best customers who are just passionate about Adidas soccer and are already talking about Adidas in social media and in forums. And we put them to work to drive sales for Adidas," says Amy Heidersbach, Needle's chief marketing officer.

Using a live chat function on the company website, potential customers are connected with Needle-powered advocates, real customers of the company. These advocates aren't in a call center, they are in their own living room or kitchen, working part time on a revenue share basis to spread their passion, answer questions, and direct website visitors to the best possible product.

Norwegian Cruise Line has been a Needle customer since 2012. A cruise is a big purchase festooned with uncertainty. Which ship should I book? Which itinerary? What excursions?

Barrie is a cruise expert who loves answering questions, and is one of the top-performing Needle advocates in the Norwegian Cruise Line community. Since she's been a certified Needle advocate for NCL, she has sold more than $5 million worth of cruises, according to Heidersbach. "If you are on Norwegian Cruise Line's website and are exhibiting behavior we've identified as needing help, you might see a window appear that says, 'Would you like to talk with Barrie, a cruise expert?'" she explains. "And if you click on that you are then put into a chat conversation with Barrie. And she's a real person. You can see her real photo. She can talk with you about all the cruises she's been on. And she knows the dimensions of the state rooms and how many inches are between the end of the bed and the wall. She knows it all."

Specialized Service Apps

Needle is integrated into the company website. Get Satisfaction can be included in a website, and can also be threaded into a business's Facebook page. Ratings and reviews software like Bazaarvoice also runs as a layer on top of an existing website. All these solutions embrace the protocol that customer service functionality is part of the broader company communication infrastructure. But what if it wasn't?

What if, in the same way consumers have adopted Yelp for local business reviews and TripAdvisor for travel reviews, they gravitated toward specific applications to complain and to contact companies?

George Klein believes that aligning customers and businesses in a mobile application that is purpose built to collect and address feedback yields the best possible outcomes for both parties. Klein is the founder of Peoplocity, a free mobile app that allows consumers to send a message at any time to any business to share feedback and request problem resolution. For customers, it works almost like a text message. They open the app, it locates nearby businesses, and they select the right merchant. They type their message, and it's delivered to the company immediately. Businesses can then respond to customers using an e-mail–like system. The optimal scenario, according to Klein, is that the issue is resolved quickly while the consumer is still at the location. Peoplocity also provides businesses with an in-depth analysis of what's being said and valuable trend data that can be used to proactively improve customer experiences.

Klein explains, "A manager at the end of the week might say, 'You know, that's the second time I've heard about a problem with the bathrooms. Let me search for bathrooms,' and it shows all the bathroom messages and he can see, 'Well, you know, that's always happening on Saturdays. That's when we have a different crew in here,' or, 'Geez, that's the third time someone said something nice about John. Let's make sure we give him a raise or a pat on the back and make sure we keep him,' that sort of thing."

Targeting the restaurant and bar industry, Coastr is another new application that seeks to meld customer service and high-touch customer experience.

"The restaurant industry as a whole has something like a 68 percent annual turnover rate," says Coastr's CEO, Brady Fletcher. "The staff members who know Jay Baer and what he prefers are not likely to be there next year. If you have a relationship with the bartender who always ensures that you have a seat for your favorite sporting event and then all of a sudden that bartender leaves, your loyalty to that venue is gone, too. If you don't have that personal touch point anymore, it changes your entire customer experience and that doesn't really work for the restaurant."

Coastr allows all team members, long-standing and new, to access customer history and be able to act upon it accordingly. The mobile application is powered by beacon technology that alerts the staff (armed with mobile phones and the business version of the Coastr app) that a known customer has entered the business, and displays that customer's preferences. The platform also encourages customers and staff to share photos and interact inside Coastr, creating a private social network centered on dining and nightlife.

"Coastr is where you can instant message with staff and friends and ask for recommendations," Fletcher says. "If I was on my way down to New York, for instance, and I fired up the Coastr app, I could see where my friends in New York had gone for food. So that extends it to a peer-to-peer recommendation platform."

Each time a customer enters a Coastr-enabled business, the presence is logged, as is the staff that served that customer. This creates a rich stream of data that can be used to determine previously hidden patterns of customer loyalty and service excellence. Coastr even tracks staff performance across multiple locations, useful in circumstances where a person bartends at multiple establishments, for example.

After each visit, Coastr contacts the customer through the application and asks for feedback on the food, the service, and other elements of the experience. Negative feedback is immediately sent to a manager for follow-up.

In addition to task-specific applications like Peoplocity and Coastr, advanced mobile app versions of popular reviews sites like Yelp, Trip-Advisor, Angie's List, and many more will make it even easier for customers to interact with businesses seamlessly and instantly in the near future.

Mobile Messaging Apps

Private, online messaging applications are likely to disrupt and transform the world of customer service in the next three to five years. In *The Definitive Guide to Social Customer Service,* Conversocial CEO and founder Joshua March provides an excellent overview: "Mobile messaging consists of applications that provide messaging functionality on phones and tablets delivered via data rather than SMS [text messaging]. WhatsApp and Facebook Messenger are the biggest in the West; WeChat is huge in Asia. These messaging apps are the biggest new force in communication, and still growing. The daily message volume on WhatsApp (owned by Facebook) is now 50 percent bigger than global SMS (text message) volume. Their functionality for one-to-one messaging has everything you need for service: real time, asynchronous, carrying a persistent identity and plugged into smartphone notifications. These messaging apps have the potential to become the biggest service channel for the mobile, social customer."[12]

Essentially, Facebook wants WhatsApp and Facebook Messenger to become the new e-mail.

As of 2015, anybody can use Facebook Messenger, even those who don't have an account on Facebook per se.[13] This has already appeared to spike usage, and Messenger overtook YouTube to become the second most used smartphone application among Americans, according to comScore data from 2015 (Facebook is first).[14]

Recently, I've been getting a lot of Facebook Messenger communications from people who previously would have e-mailed me.

Perhaps the same thing is happening to you. And as we saw in chapter 4, Facebook Messenger is also now being used between companies and customers in a customer service context.

Hyatt Hotels partnered with Conversocial to monitor and manage social media customer service, and the brand is embracing Facebook Messenger due to its speedy adoption, potential for near ubiquity, and its blend of public and private messaging functions.

"You no longer have to post your question on one platform only to be redirected to another," said Jaclyn Fu, product marketing manager at Conversocial. "Facebook Messenger is social customer service without compromises."[15]

WhatsApp has similar potential, and is already a behemoth, with 900 million monthly users worldwide as of September 2015.[16] By way of comparison, the much more ballyhooed Twitter has approximately 304 million monthly users.[17]

China's WeChat is attempting the same trick in Asia, and that platform not only allows for private messaging and customer support but in-app product purchases as well.

E-mail is not going to fully disappear, but it will become compartmentalized and marginalized the way that direct mail is today. Occasionally you get an actual letter in your physical mailbox, but typically what you get is promotional: catalogs and credit card offers and things of that nature, unidirectional blasts from companies to people. If Facebook is successful in their quest to move all person-to-person and person-to-company communications to Messenger and WhatsApp, e-mail will follow the same pattern as snail mail.

Young people have already made this shift. They don't use e-mail. My two teenagers never use the phone, and the only time they check e-mail is to confirm an online purchase. Otherwise it's all texting, Snapchat, Facebook Messenger, and WhatsApp. According to Aspect software, 36 percent of millennials would contact a company more frequently if they could text them.[18]

The same shift will happen to all businesses. We will be hugging our haters on WhatsApp instead of e-mail. And some organizations are already doing it today, assisted by an emerging ecosystem of software providers like Wasify and Casengo, which have developed interfaces to make it easier to use WhatsApp for real-time customer service.

The traffic police in New Delhi, India, have embraced this opportunity, and as of October 2014 can be reached through WhatsApp number 8750871493. Their WhatsApp presence provides a variety of important customer service functions, including help in locating towed vehicles and real-time traffic and route advice.

"WhatsApp is our best channel so far to reach commuters. We have a Facebook account, a telephone help line number and a Twitter account, but among them all, WhatsApp has turned out to be our best medium to interact with commuters," special commissioner of police traffic Muktesh Chander told the Indo-Asian News Service. This makes sense, given that Indians outpace the rest of Asia in social media customer service usage, with 71 percent of Indians using social media for customer service in the past year, compared with 29 percent of Japanese and 50 percent of Hong Kong residents, according to a study by American Express.[19]

Users of WhatsApp are also encouraged to send audiovisual complaints of traffic violations, unauthorized parking, faulty traffic signals, and other issues. Commissioner Chander says that WhatsApp was even able to help catch a thief after his agency received a video clip of the crime taking place. "A youth was fleeing on his motorbike after snatching a chain from a woman. Someone made a video of the incident and sent it to us on our WhatsApp number. We were able to identify the snatcher and soon arrested him," Chander said.

Chander said Delhi police have been making concerted efforts to utilize the potential of WhatsApp to reach out to the citizens and also for effective communication among themselves.

An inspector and about twenty-five traffic police officers monitor the WhatsApp help line around the clock. The WhatsApp number received 83,885 responses between October 17, 2014, and April 15, 2015, of which 7,681 were actionable complaints.[20]

WeChat works similarly to WhatsApp and is very popular in China, with more than 650 million users of the mobile messaging platform.

At the beginning of 2015, the newly created social media customer service team at HP evaluated WeChat alongside the HP customer service group dedicated to China, and mutually decided to add a WeChat presence for the brand.

HP isn't looking at WeChat as a revenue driver yet, but the ability to generate revenue while also providing real-time customer service is an intriguing option.

Kriti Kapoor, the director of social customer care at HP, was a guest on my podcast, Social Pros. She said that HP wanted to provide as much self-service as possible on WeChat, so they created easy-to-find resources to solve common issues.

"We understood that 40 percent of the time people are calling in for help because they're looking for a software driver, or where to download it, or they are looking for the closest support center, where they could go and drop off their laptop for field repair," she explained. "So within the WeChat environment we created a number of different tabs that allow customers to quickly look for [repair] centers, quickly look for software drivers that they can e-mail to themselves and install later, connect with HP support forums, or initiate a chat conversation with us at HP."[21]

In the nine months since debuting the WeChat channel, HP has attracted more than 100,000 followers to its account there, and it continues to grow rapidly.

This is just the beginning of the next shift in customer service channels and norms. There will be more apps. There will be more self-service. There will be greater customer expectations. But the fundamental principles and premises of hugging your haters remains valid regardless of what tomorrow's channel array may look like.

Afterword

Gartner says that 90 percent of companies will supply customer care through social media by 2020. And those that are already providing service in those public, onstage channels are rapidly increasing the variety of places where they are actively seeking to interact with customers.

According to Kriti Kapoor from HP, the brand now provides customer service in 130 different channels worldwide, and is constantly on the lookout for new opportunities to make customers' lives easier. We're a looooong way past just answering the phone and calling that the "customer service department."

Expectations are higher than ever, as major companies use remarkable customer experience as a marketing tool and set the bar for what's possible.

Pervasive use of mobile technology makes it easier than ever to complain, and customers also seek to connect with businesses in more and more and more venues.

Changes in demographics and corresponding consumer behavior are already impacting the balance between onstage and offstage interactions, and young people would do just about anything to avoid the telephone.

There are more haters than ever, and it requires more participation, with more vigilance, to please them.

But please them you can, and please them you should!

Feedback of any kind is a gift from your customers to you. They are going out of their way to use their time to tell you what they like, or where, in their estimation, you fall short. In short, haters are the most important group of customers you have, certainly more so than the "meh" middle who don't give you a chance to respond.

This is especially true, as we've learned, of the fast-growing group of onstage haters, who want an audience just as much as an answer. The public nature of feedback provided via social media, review sites, and discussion forums makes it doubly important. After all, in these channels customer service is a spectator sport.

I learned a lot while writing this book and in conducting the groundbreaking study with Edison Research that identified the crucial differences between onstage haters and offstage haters. I also read many other books, dozens of other research studies, and interviewed more than fifty customer service leaders whose thoughts and ideas are contained here.

But the three most important things I learned while writing *Hug Your Haters* are what I hope you learned while reading it:

> 1. *Customer service is more complicated than ever, but the formula for success is knowable and achievable.*
>
> 2. *Interacting with your customers, especially when they're upset, is 100 percent worth the effort.*
>
> 3. *You need to answer every complaint, in every channel, every time.*

I realize it may not be possible to answer every complaint immediately. But I hope you recognize that making the effort to embrace complaints will help you keep your customers. Take pride in interacting with more of your customers today than you did yesterday. That's a great place to start.

I very much hope that you will put into practice the ideas and recommendations I've included in this book. I would love to help you do just that, assisted by thousands of other readers who are embarking on a similar journey. Visit HugYourHaters.com to see how you can be part of ongoing training sessions, online workshops and seminars, and even Hug Your Haters academies that bring together people in similar industries to work on customer service best practices. And, of course, there are discounts and special offers available for readers of the book. See HugYourHaters.com for all the advantages and opportunities.

Last, in the spirit of *Hug Your Haters,* I want to know what you think of this book: what you liked, and what you didn't like as much. Of course, I would be delighted (overjoyed, really) if you would review the book online (see HugYourHaters.com/reviews to find reviews of this book). But if you want to keep it offstage, that's great, too.

Whatever you'd like to tell me about this book or about your own customer service experiences, please do so right now at jay@jaybaer .com. And I'll answer back!

Thank you for your interest in this topic, and your support of this book. The appendix that follows will give you a quick and easy way to refer back to the most important ideas and information in *Hug Your Haters.*

—*Jay Baer*
P.S. Remember the Rule of Reply Only Twice!

APPENDIX:

HUG YOUR HATERS—
AN EASY REFERENCE GUIDE

I f you've just finished reading the book, congratulations. You're well on your way to transforming how you look at feedback and how you handle onstage and offstage customer complaints. I've provided this easy reference guide so that you can quickly refresh your understanding of the key principles when needed. If you're the kind of person who flips to the back of the book right away, this reference guide will give you an idea of what's included in *Hug Your Haters*. I also have many more resources, including training workshops and academies where you can discuss these issues with your peers, at HugYourHaters.com.

Introduction

Key Points:

- Satisfaction among people who complain about business hasn't improved at all since the 1970s.

- Haters are not your problem. . . . Ignoring them is.

- Not responding *is* a response. A response that says "I don't care about you."
- Answering complaints increases customer advocacy. Not answering complaints decreases customer advocacy.

Key Data:

- 80 percent of businesses think they deliver "superior" customer service. Only 8 percent of customers agree.

CHAPTER 1: WHY YOU SHOULD EMBRACE COMPLAINTS

Key Points:

- Answering complaints provides four benefits:
  - Turns unhappy customers into neutral or happy customers
  - Creates customer advocacy
  - Gathers insights and intelligence
  - Differentiates you from your competitors—most companies aren't great at customer service, and consumers remember the few that are
- The most dangerous customers aren't haters; they are the "meh" in the middle, the dissatisfied customers who don't take the time to complain.

Key Data:

- A successful service recovery can spawn twenty times more positive word of mouth than regular advertising.
- 95 percent of unhappy customers will not complain in a way you can find.

- In B2B scenarios, customer experience will be more important than price by the year 2020.

CHAPTER 2: THE TWO TYPES OF HATERS AND THE DNA OF COMPLAINTS

Key Points:

- Offstage haters complain in private (telephone, e-mail). They are older, less mobile and technology savvy, and complain less often.
- Offstage haters want an answer.
- Onstage haters complain in public (social media, review websites, discussion forums). They are younger, mobile and tech savvy, and complain more often.
- Onstage haters want an audience.

Key Data:

- In 2015, 62 percent of first complaints were made via telephone or e-mail.
- The more active people are in social media, the more likely they are to be heavy complainers.

CHAPTER 3: THE HATRIX: WHO COMPLAINS, WHERE, AND WHY

Key Points:

- Offstage haters almost always expect a response.
- Fewer than half of onstage haters expect a response.
- The greatest increase in customer advocacy comes when you respond to haters who do not expect a response (onstage, primarily).

Key Data:

- Approximately two-thirds of offstage haters are satisfied with phone and e-mail response times.

- One-third of onstage haters are satisfied with social media response time.

- 39 percent of social media complainers expect a response within one hour, yet the average response time by businesses (when they respond at all) is five hours.

- 71 percent of social media complaints are logged on Facebook.

- 80 percent of American consumers say they trust online reviews as much as personal recommendations.

CHAPTER 4: CUSTOMER SERVICE IS A SPECTATOR SPORT

Key Points:

- Onstage haters and public channels for interaction may eventually outnumber offstage haters and private channels.

- Young people are uncomfortable using the telephone and e-mail, the primary offstage communication channels.

- When handled poorly, offstage haters can become onstage haters.

- Hugging your haters doesn't mean the customer is always right, but it does mean the customer is always answered.

Key Data:

- In the UK, two-thirds of people who have used social media for customer support now prefer it to a traditional call center.

- Handling a customer in social media costs less than $1.00, compared to $2.50–$5.00 to interact through e-mail, and more than $6.00 to provide telephone support (per call).

- In the Netherlands, 71 percent of all online complaints occur because of a failure in traditional customer service.

- More than two-thirds of customers trust reviews more when they see both positive and negative reviews.

CHAPTER 5: BIG BUTS: 5 OBSTACLES TO PROVIDING GREAT SERVICE

Key Points:

- There are five reasons businesses and organizations do not answer every complaint, in every channel, every time. Each of these obstacles must be overcome to hug your haters effectively:
  - There are too many channels.
  - There is too much feedback.
  - You take complaints personally.
  - You fear getting scammed.
  - You don't have a customer service culture.

Key Data:

- In the UK, there was an eightfold increase in social media complaints between January 2014 and May 2015.

- A 5 percent increase in customer retention can boost profits by 25 to 85 percent.

- Globally, $500 billion is invested each year in marketing, compared to $9 billion in customer service.

CHAPTER 6: H-O-U-R-S: THE PLAYBOOK FOR HUGGING OFFSTAGE HATERS

Key Points:

- The five key points to remember when dealing with offstage haters:
    - be **Human**
    - use **One** channel
    - **Unify** your data
    - and **Resolve** the issue
    - with **Speed**

Key Data:

- Getting the issue solved in a single transaction is more important to a customer than accuracy or politeness.
- Customers receiving a successful first-contact problem resolution are twice as likely to buy from the company again.
- 85 percent of customers feel negative when they have to provide information multiple times.

CHAPTER 7: F-E-A-R-S: THE PLAYBOOK FOR HUGGING ONSTAGE HATERS

Key Points:

- The five key points to remember when dealing with onstage haters:
    - **Find** all mentions
    - display **Empathy**
    - **Answer** publicly

- Reply only twice
- Switch channels

- The Rule of Reply Only Twice: Never respond more than twice to the same customer about the same issue in a public channel.

Key Data:

- One-third of all tweets about companies are for customer service, but only 3 percent include the company's Twitter username with the @ handle.
- More than 60 percent of businesses say they are incapable of handling customer service issues in one contact in social media.

CHAPTER 8: THE FUTURE OF CUSTOMER SERVICE

Key Points:

- The five emerging trends that will disrupt and transform customer service and customer experience (beyond the rise of onstage haters):
    - Proactive customer service
    - Self-service
    - Community-based service
    - Specialized service apps
    - Mobile messaging apps
- You must interact with your customers in the venues of their choosing, not only the venues you prefer.

Key Data:

- 72 percent of customers prefer using a company's website to answer their questions.

- Community support can decrease customer service costs by 10 to 50 percent.

- 36 percent of millennials would contact companies more frequently if they could do so with a text message.

ACKNOWLEDGMENTS

Awork like *Hug Your Haters* is truly a team effort. Thank you to my family for your incredible support of this book, and of my previous publications. It's hard when Dad goes into book-writing mode and disappears into the basement. I love you for (among many other things) understanding my occasional absences and mental distractions.

Thanks as well to my amazing team at Convince & Convert, who deliver world-class advice and counsel to some of the planet's most interesting companies. Your dedication and commitment inspire me every day.

Special hugs and high-fives to my research assistant, Kristina Paider. She used her extensive skills as a professional screenwriter to help shape the narrative and structure of *Hug Your Haters*. Kristina's fingerprints are all over this book.

An enormous thank-you to my literary agent, Jim Levine, and to the entire team at Portfolio, especially my very patient and encouraging editor, Natalie Horbachevsky, and editorial assistant, the intriguingly named Merry Sun.

I also very much appreciate the wisdom, time, and candor of the fifty-plus people interviewed for this book. Without you, there would be no *Hug Your Haters*.

Finally—but perhaps most important—thank you to the crazy fans who purchased multiple copies of this book before it was even written. You are the opposite of haters! Thanks to Chris Mikulin, NOW Marketing Group, Rachel Miller, Dave Wells, Susan McLennan, Carrie Gallagher, Ginny Langan, Janice Person, Doug Karr, Jared DiVincent, Dawn Beasley, Chelsea Worldwide, Stephanie Kashdan, Michelle Marostica, Jon Steiert, Jeff DeHaven, Michelle McCullough, Thomas Muraca, Stephanie Riel, Camara Lewis, Ben Miller, Kathryn Zimmerman, Ken Chandler, Jody Conley, Richard Stuart, Danielle Antosz, Maggie Young, Jeremy Cady, Jimmy Smith, Jr., Brandon Steiner, Jill Nicholson, and Peter Gailey.

AUTHOR'S NOTE

This book is all about the power of feedback. So, of course, I want yours!

I would love your review of this book, too, on the website of your favorite bookseller, on social media (I'm @jaybaer on Twitter), or via e-mail (jay@jaybaer.com). I'll respond to every one of them!

To see all reviews of *Hug Your Haters*, go to HugYourHaters .com/reviews.

GET MORE HUG YOUR HATERS

And remember, the website has all sorts of resources to help you put these principles in practice. Webinars, training courses, free bonus material that wouldn't fit into this book. Even an online community of people in customer service and customer experience working together to find the best possible solution to handling haters—especially the onstage ones. Join us over there, won't you? See you at HugYourHaters.com.

HUG YOUR HATERS AT YOUR COMPANY OR EVENT

My team at Convince & Convert and I provide practical, useful consulting, training workshops, audits, competitive analyses, and keynote speeches for companies and organizations worldwide. We can help you improve your customer service and customer experience; visit ConvinceAndConvert.com for details.

NOTES

Introduction

1. John Tschohl, "Companies Don't See Reality in Their Service Reflection," Service Quality Institute, March 21, 2013, http://www
   .customer-service.com/blog/201303/companies_misunderstand
   _what_customers_want (accessed September 7, 2015).
2. Ibid.
3. Arizona State University, "Will We Ever Learn? The Sad State of
   Customer Care in America," Customer Care MC, November 2013,
   http://www.customercaremc.com/wp/wp-content/uploads/2014/
   01/KeyFindingsFrom2013NationalCustomerRageSurvey.pdf
   (accessed September 7, 2015).
4. Jay Z., "White Castle in Cicero, IL," Yelp, August 11, 2008, http://
   www.yelp.com/biz/white-castle-cicero?hrid=GU232Z7i7ezHiJ
   _l9URvrQ (accessed September 7, 2015).

Chapter 1: Why You Should Embrace Complaints

1. Ray S., "Fresh Brothers Pizza in Hollywood Hills, CA," Yelp,
   April 10, 2014, http://www.yelp.com/biz/fresh-brothers-holly

wood?hrid=rGCtkl7dq0LF-sMf-fN0_Q& (accessed September 7, 2015).

2. Debbie Goldberg, "Fresh Brothers Pizza in Hollywood Hills, CA." Yelp, August 29, 2014, http://www.yelp.com/biz/fresh-brothers -hollywood?hrid=rGCtkl7dq0LF-sMf-fN0_Q& (accessed September 7, 2015).

3. Chris V., "Fresh Brothers Pizza, Hollywood Hills, CA," Yelp, April 28, 2015, http://www.yelp.com/biz/fresh-brothers-hollywood?hrid =BCyG-1uCaY_dgGVykRwtiw (accessed September 7, 2015).

4. Debbie Goldberg, "Fresh Brothers Pizza in Hollywood Hills, CA," Yelp, May 8, 2015, http://www.yelp.com/biz/fresh-brothers -hollywood?hrid=BCyG-1uCaY_dgGVykRwtiw (accessed September 7, 2015).

5. Bente Lilja Bye, "Volcanic Eruptions: Science and Risk Management," *Science 2.0,* May 27, 2011, http://www.science20.com/planetbye/ volcanic_eruptions_science_and_risk_management-79456 (accessed September 7, 2015).

6. Shaun Smith, "Marketing Is a Tax You Pay for Being Unremarkable," *Customer Think,* April 1, 2008, http://customerthink.com/marketing _tax_being_unremarkable/ (accessed September 7, 2015).

7. Janelle Barlow and Claus Moller, *A Complaint Is a Gift: Recovering Customer Loyalty When Things Go Wrong* (San Francisco: Berrett-Koehler, 2008), Kindle edition.

8. Frederick F. Reichheld and W. Earl Sasser Jr., "Zero Defections: Quality Comes to Services," *Harvard Business Review,* October 1990, https://hbr.org/1990/09/zero-defections-quality-comes-to -services/ar/1 (accessed September 7, 2015).

9. http://gawker.com/british-writer-tracks-down-teen-who-gave -his-book-a-bad-1741713016?utm_expid=66866090-62 .YkETBcIMTk2uX1oytHipyg.0.

10. Jacob Sapochnick, "The Social Landscape of 2015: Reflection on SMMW 2015," *Enchanting Lawyer,* April 6, 2015, http://www .enchantinglawyer.com/social-landscape/ (accessed September 7, 2015).

11. Andrew P. Turko, "Email to Tim Cook Regarding the Launch," *MacRumors,* April 10, 2015, http://forums.macrumors.com/showthread.php?t=1865424 (accessed September 7, 2015).

12. Guy Winch, *The Squeaky Wheel: Complaining the Right Way to Get Results, Improve Your Relationships, and Enhance Self-Esteem* (New York: Walker Publishing Company, 2011), Kindle edition.

13. Ibid.

14. Rob Markey and Fred Reichheld, "The Economics of Loyalty," *Bain & Company,* March 23, 2012, http://www.bain.com/publications/articles/the-economics-of-loyalty.aspx (accessed September 7, 2015).

15. Rob Speciale, Twitter, March 11, 2013, https://twitter.com/RobSpeciale/status/311297618389127168 (accessed September 7, 2015).

16. Discover Financial Services, Twitter, March 11, 2013, https://twitter.com/Discover/status/311299872328384512 (accessed September 7, 2015).

17. Rob Speciale, Twitter, March 11, 2013, https://twitter.com/RobSpeciale/status/311300980841017344 (accessed September 7, 2015).

18. Peter Shankman, *Zombie Loyalists* (New York: St. Martin's Press, 2015), Kindle edition.

19. Winch, *The Squeaky Wheel: Complaining the Right Way to Get Results, Improve Your Relationships, and Enhance Self-Esteem* (New York: Walker Publishing Company, 2011), Kindle edition.

20. Mary Shulzhenko, "*Customers 2020: The Future of B-to-B Customer Experience (Infographic),*" *Provide Support* (blog), April 2, 2015, http://www.providesupport.com/blog/customers-2020-infographic/ (accessed September 7, 2015).

21. *Customers 2020: The Future of B-to-B Customer Experience,* Walker, http://www.walkerinfo.com/Customers2020/ (accessed September 10, 2015).

22. John R. DiJulius III, *The Customer Service Revolution: Overthrow Conventional Business, Inspire Employees, and Change the World* (Austin, TX: Greenleaf Book Group Press, 2015), Kindle edition.

Chapter 2: **The Two Types of Haters and the DNA of Complaints**

1. "2014 State of Multichannel Customer Service Survey," Parature, 2014, http://ww2.parature.com/lp/report-2014-state-multichannel -cs-survey-comm.html (accessed September 10, 2015).

2. FlashAndFilm, "Consumer Calls Jimmy Dean with Sausage Complaint," YouTube, January 5, 2011, https://www.youtube.com/ watch?v=7CuXf2iMem0 (accessed September 7, 2015).

3. "Extreme Customer Expectations Have Gone Global," *Lithium,* October 15, 2014, http://www.lithium.com/company/news-room/ press-releases/2014/extreme-customer-expectations-have-gone -global (accessed September 7, 2015).

4. Ibid.

5. Olga Ter Voert, "Complaints on Social Media (and How to Minimise the Damage They Cause)," TNS NIPO, November 28, 2013, http:// www.slideshare.net/oursocialtimes/complaints-on-social-media -and-how-to-minimise-the-damage-they-cause-olga-ter-voert-tns -nipo (accessed September 7, 2015).

6. Guy Winch, *The Squeaky Wheel.*

7. Gotta Kid to Feed, "Real Actors Read Yelp," YouTube, February 14, 2013, https://www.youtube.com/watch?v=FUV7GH4Qidc (accessed September 7, 2015).

8. Mandi Woodruff, "Here's How Much It Cost a British Airways Customer to Blast the Company in Promoted Tweets," *Business Insider,* September 4, 2013, http://www.businessinsider.com/hasan -syed-spent-1000-to-blast-british-airways-on-twitter-2013-9 (accessed September 7, 2015).

9. Alyson Shontell, "Angry Customer Buys Promoted Tweets to Bash British Airways for Losing His Luggage," *Business Insider,* September 3, 2013, http://www.businessinsider.com/customer-buys-promoted -tweets-to-bash-british-airways-2013-9 (accessed September 7, 2015).

10. Kabir Chibber, "Science Can Now Spot Trolls After Just Five Horrible, Malicious Comments," *Quartz,* April 19, 2015, http://

qz.com/386694/science-can-now-spot-trolls-after-just-five
-horrible-malicious-comments/ (accessed September 7, 2015).

11. Matt Weinberger, "Twitter Is Testing a Tool to Zap Hate Speech," *Business Insider,* March 23, 2015, http://www.businessinsider .com/twitter-is-testing-a-tool-to-zap-hate-speech-2015-3 (accessed September 7, 2015).

12. "Most Responsive Brand on Twitter," Guinness World Records, http://www.guinnessworldrecords.com/world-records/most -responsive-brand-on-twitter/ (accessed September 10, 2015).

Chapter 3: The Hatrix: Who Complains, Where, and Why

1. "About Net Promoter," Satmetrix, Net Promoter Community, http://www.netpromoter.com/why-net-promoter/about-net -promoter (accessed September 10, 2015).

2. "Local Consumer Review Study 2015," BrightLocal, https:// www.brightlocal.com/learn/local-consumer-review-survey/ (accessed September 10, 2015).

3. "Extreme Customer Expectations Have Gone Global," *Lithium*, October 15, 2014, http://www.lithium.com/company/news-room/ press-releases/2014/extreme-customer-expectations-have-gone -global (accessed September 7, 2015).

Chapter 4: Customer Service Is a Spectator Sport

1. Fishburn Hedges and Echo Research, "The Social Media Customer," Institute of Customer Service, https://www.instituteofcustomerservice .com/files/The_social_media_customer_by_Fishburn_Hedges.pdf (accessed September 11, 2015).

2. Gadi Benmark and Dan Singer, "Turn Customer Care into 'Social Care' to Break Away from the Competition," *Harvard Business Review,* December 19, 2012, https://hbr.org/2012/12/turn-customer -care-into-social/ (accessed September 11, 2015).

3. Olga Ter Voert, "Complaints on Social Media (and How to Minimise the Damage They Cause)." TNS NIPO, November 28,

2013, http://www.slideshare.net/oursocialtimes/complaints-on -social-media-and-how-to-minimise-the-damage-they-cause-olga -ter-voert-tns-nipo (accessed September 7, 2015).

4. Priscilla Jones's profile on Spiceworks, http://community.spice works.com/people/priscilla-hp (accessed September 11, 2015).

5. Chris Gillis and Priscilla Jones, "HP P4515X Has an Identity Issue," Spiceworks, http://community.spiceworks.com/topic/953926-hp -p4515x-has-an-identity-issue (accessed September 11, 2015).

6. Hotel 41 profile page, TripAdvisor, http://www.tripadvisor.com/ Hotel_Review-g186338-d188961-Reviews-Hotel_41-London _England.html#REVIEWS (accessed September 11, 2015).

7. Douglas L., "Service Beyond Any Expectation," TripAdvisor, June 16, 2015, http://www.tripadvisor.com/ShowUserReviews-g186338 -d188961-r280686288-Hotel_41-London_England.html# (accessed September 11, 2015).

8. Bill Tancer, *Everyone's a Critic* (New York: Portfolio, 2014), Kindle edition.

9. Wendy Davis, "Yelp Takes Aim at Fake Review Purveyors," *Online Media Daily,* February 17, 2015, http://www.mediapost.com/ publications/article/243957/yelp-takes-aim-at-fake-review -purveyors.html# (accessed September 11, 2015).

10. WanderingRoots and Murray Waters, TripAdvisor, http://www .tripadvisor.com/ShowUserReviews-g155043-d188301-r120803621 -Ramada_Saskatoon-Saskatoon_Saskatchewan.html (accessed September 11, 2015).

11. Chef John Howie, "Let's See If We Can't Fix That Experience for Her," YouTube, June 11, 2009, https://www.youtube.com/watch ?v=iaRkLPQHGLg&feature=youtu.be (accessed September 11, 2015).

12. Primrose Riordan, "Sarah Hanson-Young Reads Out 'Mean Tweets' in New Video," *Sydney Morning Herald,* March 19, 2015, http:// www.smh.com.au/federal-politics/political-news/sarah -hansonyoung-reads-out-mean-tweets-in-new-video-20150319 -1m2sww.html (accessed September 11, 2015).

13. Joe Mullin, "FTC Busts Auto-Shipping Company for Its Discounts-for-Reviews Deal," *Ars Technica,* April 20, 2015, http://arstechnica.com/tech-policy/2015/04/20/ftc-busts-auto-shipping-company-for-its-discounts-for-reviews-deal/ (accessed September 11, 2015).

14. Tancer, *Everyone's a Critic.*

15. Will Cook, "Grade DC: How Citizen Feedback Is Changing Service Delivery," *Government Technology,* October 16, 2013, http:// www.govtech.com/data/Grade-DC-How- Citizen-Feedback-Is-Changing-Service-Delivery.html (accessed September 11, 2015).

16. "Bad Reviews Are Good for Business," Reevoo, eBook, 2013, https://www.reevoo.com/resources/bad-reviews-are-good-for-business/ (accessed September 11, 2015).

17. Conversocial, *The Definitive Guide to Social Customer Service, 2015 edition,* http://cdn2.hubspot.net/hubfs/154001/The_Definitive_Guide_to_Social_Customer_Service_2015.pdf (accessed September 11, 2015).

18. Todd Kron, Twitter, https://twitter.com/Shutterstock/status/56808 4567485255680 (accessed September 11, 2015).

19. Suzanne Deveney, Twitter, https://twitter.com/soozed/status/5680 97544787644417 (accessed September 11, 2015).

20. Cade Metz, "Twitter Now Lets Total Strangers Direct-Message You," *Wired,* April 20, 2015, http://www.wired.com/2015/04/twitter-allows-direct-messages-people-dont-follow/ (accessed September 11, 2015).

21. uShip, Facebook page member support application, https://www.facebook.com/uShip/app_267506003363207 (accessed September 11, 2015).

22. Jillian D'Onfro, "Facebook Made a Huge Move This Week That Could Lead to Its Next Billion-Dollar Business," *Business Insider,* June 27, 2015, http://www.businessinsider.com/why-facebook-messenger-is-big-business-for-facebook-2015-6 (accessed September 11, 2015).

Chapter 5: **Big Buts: 5 Obstacles to Providing Great Service**

1. "2014 State of Multichannel Customer Service Survey," Parature.

2. Customers 2020, Walker.

3. Joe Causon, "Customer Complaints Made Via Social Media on the Rise," *Guardian*, May 21, 2015, http://www.theguardian.com/media-network/2015/may/21/customer-complaints-social-media-rise?CMP=new_1194&CMP (accessed September 11, 2015).

4. Andrea Ayers, "Why Customer Service Jobs Will Grow and Grow," *Forbes*, February 25, 2010, http://www.forbes.com/2010/02/25/customer-service-jobs-leadership-managing-marketing.html (accessed September 11, 2015).

5. Conversocial, *Definitive Guide to Social Customer Service.*

6. DiJulius III, *Customer Service Revolution.*

7. "Umpqua Holdings Corporation," Wikipedia, http://en.wikipedia.org/wiki/Umpqua_Holdings_Corporation (accessed September 11, 2015).

8. Barlow and Moller, *A Complaint Is a Gift.*

9. Cheryl Lin Rodsted, Instagram, https://instagram.com/p/1ewXhJPAZ1/ (accessed September 14, 2015).

10. Ibid.

11. Judith E. Glaser and Richard D. Glaser, "The Neurochemistry of Positive Conversations," *Harvard Business Review*, June 12, 2014, https://hbr.org/2014/06/the-neurochemistry-of-positive-conversations/ (accessed September 14, 2015).

12. Ibid.

13. Lee Cockerell, *The Customer Rules: The 39 Essential Rules for Delivering Sensational Service* (New York: Crown Business, 2013), Kindle edition.

14. "'Subaru for the Win!' Dealership Hits Back at Union Protest with Kick-Ass Sign," Twitchy, March 14, 2014, http://twitchy.com/2014/03/14/subaru-for-the-win-dealership-hits-back-at-union-protest-with-kick-ass-sign-pics-video/ (accessed September 14, 2015).

15. "Social Commerce: Bad Reviews Are Good for Business," Reevoo, February 11, 2002, https://www.reevoo.com/news/social-commerce -bad-reviews-are-good-for-business/ (accessed September 14, 2015).

16. Daniel Lemin, *Manipurated: How Business Owners Can Fight Fraudulent Online Ratings and Reviews* (Fresno, CA: Quill Driver Books, 2015), advance electronic copy.

17. Mara Siegler, "Hotel Fines $500 for Every Bad Review Posted Online," *New York Post,* Page Six, August 4, 2014, http://pagesix .com/2014/08/04/hotel-charges-500-for-every-bad-review -posted-online/ (accessed September 14, 2015).

18. Amy Langfield, "Hotel's $500 'Joke' Led to 3,000 Bad Reviews," *Today,* August 5, 2014, http://www.today.com/news/union-street -guest-houses-500-joke-led-3-000-bad-1D80024902 (accessed September 14, 2015).

19. Rabith Z, Yelp, November 21, 2013, http://www.yelp.com/biz/ union-street-guest-house-hudson?hrid=_p-R59VY-c19Nmxt 4r9X9w (accessed September 14, 2015).

20. Cockerell, *The Customer Rules.*

21. Reichheld and Sasser, "Zero Defections."

22. Luke Brynley-Jones, "Can Customer Service Deliver a Higher ROI Than Marketing?" *Our Social Times,* September 18, 2014, http://oursocialtimes.com/can-customer-service-deliver-a-higher -roi-than-marketing/ (accessed September 14, 2015).

23. Frank Eliason, @ *Your Service: How to Attract New Customers, Increase Sales, and Grow Your Business Using Simple Customer Service Techniques* (Hoboken, NJ: Wiley, 2012), Kindle edition.

24. Matthew Dixon, Karen Freeman, and Nicholas Toman, "Stop Trying to Delight Your Customers," *Harvard Business Review,* July–August 2010, https://hbr.org/2010/07/stop-trying-to-delight -your-customers (accessed September 14, 2015).

Chapter 6: H-O-U-R-S: The Playbook for Hugging Offstage Haters

1. Steve Curtin, "Delta Connections," *Steve Curtin Customer Enthusiast* (blog), February 25, 2011, http://www.stevecurtin.com/blog/2011/02/15/delta-connections/ (accessed September 14, 2015).

2. Dixon, Freeman, and Toman, "Stop Trying to Delight Your Customers."

3. Cynthia J. Grimm, "When to Offer Fewer Customer Service Channels," *Harvard Business Review,* May 19, 2015, https://hbr.org/2015/05/when-to-offer-fewer-customer-service-channels (accessed September 14, 2015).

4. Barlow and Moller, *A Complaint Is a Gift.*

5. Dixon, Freeman, and Toman, "Stop Trying to Delight Your Customers," http://www.nedbankgroup.co.za/financials/2008Sustainability/pdf/Section%204.pdf.

6. Thunderhead.com and Populus Research, "Engagement 3.0: A New Model for Customer Engagement," February 2014, https://hmn-uploads-eu.s3.amazonaws.com/thunderhead-production/uploads/2014/02/Engagement_3-0_US_Report-PDF-web.pdf (accessed September 14, 2015).

7. Ibid.

8. Cockerell, *The Customer Rules.*

9. Helen Leggatt, "Email Customer Service Response Times Lengthen, Twitter Improves," *BizReport.* March 23, 2015, http://www.bizreport.com/2015/03/email-customer-service-response-times-lengthen-twitter-impro.html (accessed September 14, 2015).

10. "2014 State of Multichannel Customer Service Survey," Parature.

Chapter 7: F-E-A-R-S: The Playbook for Hugging Onstage Haters

1. Drew Hester, Twitter, May 16, 2015, https://twitter.com/drewhester12/status/599648186031087618 (accessed September 14, 2015).

2. Indy Motor Speedway, Twitter, May 16, 2015, https://twitter.com/IMS/status/599648720326529026 (accessed September 14, 2015).

3. Conversocial, *Definitive Guide to Social Customer Service.*

4. Harry Mills, PhD, "Physiology of Anger," *MentalHelp.net,* June 25, 2015, https://www.mentalhelp.net/articles/physiology-of-anger/ (accessed September 14, 2015).

5. Scott Stratten, Twitter, October 9, 2014, https://twitter.com/unmarketing/status/520378536730050560 (accessed September 14, 2015).

6. Spotify, Twitter, October 10, 2014, https://twitter.com/SpotifyCares/status/520586270545043456 (accessed September 14, 2015).

7. Scott Stratten, Twitter, October 10, 2014, https://twitter.com/unmarketing/status/520587938154160128 (accessed September 14, 2015).

8. Grimm, "When to Offer Fewer Customer Service Channels."

9. Manitoba Telecom Services' Facebook page, June 11, 2015, https://www.facebook.com/MTSTalks/posts/1079156565445293:0 (accessed September 14, 2015).

10. Ibid.

11. Subway's Facebook page, May 22, 2015, https://www.facebook.com/subway/posts/10153392648904974:0 (accessed September 14, 2015).

12. Ibid.

13. Anthony Ha, "More Than Half a Billion People Access Facebook Solely from Mobile," *TechCrunch,* January 28, 2015, http://techcrunch.com/2015/01/28/facebook-mobile-only-2/ (accessed September 14, 2015).

14. Whitney Fowler, Twitter, December 18, 2014, https://twitter.com/whitlash/status/545657613741199360 (accessed September 14, 2015).

15. Warby Parker, Twitter, December 18, 2014, https://twitter.com/WarbyParker/status/545684354044006400 (accessed September 14, 2015).

Chapter 8: **The Future of Customer Service**

1. *Customers 2020*, Walker.

2. Neil Davey, "Self-Service Warning: Why You Can Still Lose in a Win-Win Game," *MyCustomer,* July 3, 2014, http://www.mycustomer.com/feature/experience/can-anything-derail-self-service-revolution/167451 (accessed September 14, 2015).

3. Ibid.

4. Ibid.

5. Holiday World website, http://www.holidayworld.com/rides/thunderbirdsteelrollercoaster/ (accessed September 14, 2015).

6. Jay Baer, *Youtility: Why Smart Marketing Is About Help Not Hype* (New York: Portfolio, 2013), Kindle edition.

7. Holiday World & Splashin' Safari reviews, TripAdvisor, http://www.tripadvisor.com/Attraction_Review-g37506-d126379-eviews-Holiday_World_Splashin_Safari-Santa_Claus_Indiana.html#REVIEWS (accessed September 14, 2015).

8. Baer, *Youtility.*

9. Aspect and the Center for Generational Kinetics, "The Aspect Consumer Experience Index: Millennial Research on Customer Service Expectations," 2015, http://www.aspect.com/millennials (accessed September 14, 2015).

10. Gartner, "Gartner Says Organizations That Integrate Communities into Customer Support Can Realize Cost Reductions of Up to 50 Percent," press release, February 21, 2012, http://www.gartner.com/newsroom/id/1929014 (accessed September 14, 2015).

11. Vision Critical, "Vision Critical Customer Stories: STM," https://www.visioncritical.com/customer-stories/stm/ (accessed September 14, 2015).

12. Conversocial, *Definitive Guide to Social Customer Service.*

13. Josh Constine, "Messenger No Longer Requires a Facebook Account," *TechCrunch,* June 24, 2015, http://techcrunch.com/2015/06/24/nobook-messenger/ (accessed September 14, 2015).

14. Aslam F. Zaveeth, "Facebook Messenger Overtakes YouTube in US App Popularity," *The Next Digit,* September 6, 2015, http://thenextdigit.com/25992/facebook-messenger-overtakes-youtube-app-popularity/ (accessed September 14, 2105).

15. http://digiday.com/brands/hyatt-takes-customer-service-facebook-messenger/.

16. "Number of Monthly Active WhatsApp Users Worldwide from April 2013 to September 2015," Statista, http://www.statista.com/statistics/260819/number-of-monthly-active-whatsapp-users/ (accessed September 14, 2015).

17. "Number of Monthly Active Twitter Users Worldwide from 1st Quarter 2010 to 2nd Quarter 2015," Statista, http://www.statista.com/statistics/282087/number-of-monthly-active-twitter-users/ (accessed September 14, 2015).

18. Aspect and the Center for Generational Kinetics, "The Aspect Consumer Experience Index."

19. "71% Indians Use Social Media to Get Customer Service Response," http:// m.firstpost.com/ business/ 71-indians- use- social -media-to-get-customer-service-response-2471304.html.

20. Indo-Asian News Service, "Now Delhi Police WhatsApp to Give Information on Towed Vehicle," NDTV, April 19, 2015, http://www.ndtv.com/delhi-news/now-delhi-police-whatsapp-to-give-information-on-towed-vehicles-756289 (accessed September 14, 2015).

21. "How HP Balances Social Marketing with Social Customer Service," http://www.convinceandconvert.com/podcasts/episodes/how-hp-balances-social-marketing-with-social-customer-service/.

INDEX

Note: Page numbers in *italics* refer to graphs and charts.

ABOUT THE AUTHOR

Jay Baer is the president of Convince & Convert, an online customer service and digital marketing consultancy and media company that advises some of the most iconic organizations in the world,
including the United Nations, Oracle, and TaylorMade Adidas Golf.

Jay is the *New York Times* best-selling author of five books,
including *Youtility: Why Smart Marketing Is About Help Not Hype*.

The most retweeted person in the world among digital marketers, Jay writes for *Inc., Entrepreneur,* and *Forbes* magazines online,
and he owns the world's number one content marketing blog and
produces multiple award-winning podcasts. His longest-running
show, Social Pros, was named best marketing podcast in the 2015
Content Marketing Awards.

Jay is an avid tequila collector and father of two. He currently resides
in Bloomington, Indiana. Find him online at ConvinceAndConvert
.com, jaybaer.com, and @jaybaer on Twitter.